Praise for *Animal ER*

"Intriguing . . . exhilarating."
—*The Boston Globe*

"A breath-bating glimpse of animals in medical peril and the very beautiful
emergency room choreography of those who attend to them."
—*Kirkus Reviews*

"Heartwarming."
—*Library Journal*

"A riveting in-the-trenches portrait . . . refreshing and captivating . . .
Leaves you with an unquenchable yearning for more."
—*The Seattle Times*

"Drink up every word in this well-written book."
—*St. Paul Pioneer Press*

"Captivating . . . A moving testament to the healing power of medicine
and love, and the special bond that exists between animals and people."
—*St. Louis Post-Dispatch*

"*Animal ER* delivers heart-stopping action."
—*Dog Fancy*

"*Animal ER* is a book you just won't put down."
—*Pasadena Star-News*

"Each story reads like a front-page scoop. Perilous emergency situations,
heroic life-saving measures, and compassion meld with insight
into the thought processes of the veterinarians intent on
providing maximum care, often against all odds."
—*The Sunday Star-Ledger* (Newark, New Jersey)

The Tufts University School of Veterinary Medicine has the country's
largest residency training program in animal emergency medicine and critical
care. It treats more than 24,000 animals a year and ranks among the top veterinary schools in the United States.

Vicki Croke is a columnist for the *Boston Globe* and the author of *The
Modern Ark: The Story of Zoos—Past, Present, and Future.*

THE TUFTS UNIVERSITY
SCHOOL OF VETERINARY MEDICINE
WITH VICKI CROKE

ANIMAL ER

EXTRAORDINARY STORIES OF
HOPE AND HEALING FROM
ONE OF THE WORLD'S LEADING
VETERINARY HOSPITALS

A PLUME BOOK

PLUME
Published by the Penguin Group
Penguin Putnam Inc., 375 Hudson Street, New York, New York 10014, U.S.A.
Penguin Books Ltd, 27 Wrights Lane, London W8 5TZ, England
Penguin Books Australia Ltd, Ringwood, Victoria, Australia
Penguin Books Canada Ltd, 10 Alcorn Avenue, Toronto, Ontario, Canada M4V 3B2
Penguin Books (N.Z.) Ltd, 182–190 Wairau Road, Auckland 10, New Zealand

Penguin Books Ltd, Registered Offices: Harmondsworth, Middlesex, England

Published by Plume, a member of Penguin Putnam Inc. Previously published in a
Dutton edition.

First Plume Printing, November 2000
10 9 8 7 6 5 4 3 2 1

 REGISTERED TRADEMARK—MARCA REGISTRADA

The Library of Congress has catalogued the Dutton edition as follows:
Tufts University. School of Veterinary Medicine.
    Animal er : extraordinary stories of hope and healing from one of the world's
leading veterinary hospitals / The Tufts University School of Veterinary Medicine
with Vicki Croke.
        p.   cm.
    ISBN 0-525-94507-5 (hc.)
            0-452-28101-6 (pbk.)
    1. Foster Hospital for Small Animals (Medford, Mass.) Anecdotes. 2. Veterinary
emergencies—Massachusetts—Medford Anecdotes. 3. Animals—Massachusetts—
Medford Anecdotes.   I. Croke, Vicki.   II. Title.
SF604.62.M42F678   1999
636.08'32—dc21   99-32017
                                                                            CIP

Printed in the United States of America
Original hardcover design by Eve L. Kirch

BOOKS ARE AVAILABLE AT QUANTITY DISCOUNTS WHEN USED TO PROMOTE PRODUCTS OR SER-
VICES. FOR INFORMATION PLEASE WRITE TO PREMIUM MARKETING DIVISION, PENGUIN PUTNAM
INC., 375 HUDSON STREET, NEW YORK, NEW YORK 10014.

Contents

ACKNOWLEDGMENTS

THERE is simply no way to properly thank everyone at the Tufts University School of Medicine who helped me receive the Cliff Notes version of a veterinary education.

First, great thanks go to Dr. Nicholas Dodman, who masterminded the entire project. He is brilliant, quick-witted, and insightful. I'm honored to have gotten the chance to work with him.

Nick made sure all doors were open to me, and several people helped guide me through them. Judy Hall of the Dean's Office knows all and can get anything done. She is also a dear friend. Patricia Methot and Ronni Tinker of the hospital staff were always available and happy to help.

To all the talented technicians in the ICU, thank you for your help and good humor.

In order to capture the essence of the ICU, I was allowed to shadow, and question, veterinarians through every phase of treating patients—from first examination to X-ray, to surgery, and post-operative care in the intensive care unit. The residents and one intern, with whom I spent the most time, lost a

lot of privacy but never their patience, and I am extremely grateful to Carolyn Garzotto, Alison Gaynor, Ari Jutkowitz, Armelle
de Laforcade, John MacGregor, Maureen McMichael, Steve
Mensack, Jana Norris, Lisa Powell, and Gretchen Schoeffler.

Two of these doctors in particular became pals: Gretchen—
who often would get so involved in her cases so quickly that
she would leave me stranded in the hallway, forgetting to ask
the client in the examining room if I could come in. Gretchen,
all is forgiven. And Maureen McMichael, a wonderful veterinarian who is never afraid to explore the deeply philosophical aspect of any issue.

Through the trauma and drama of the ICU, the commitment and compassion of these veterinarians is as ceaseless as
it is stunning.

Thanks also to Dr. Mark Pokras and everyone in Wildlife.
To Dr. John Berg, department head of clinical sciences, and
exotics vet Dr. Rose Borkowski. Dr. Carl Kirker-Head, of the
large animal hospital. And the indispensable Margaret Combs
of the press office.

And to Dean Philip Kosch who has enough faith in his
school to let a journalist loose with no restrictions in the
hospital.

Thanks also to my editor at Dutton, Jennifer Dickerson Ka-
sius, who dealt with tight deadlines for this manuscript with
the nerves of steel of an emergency-room doctor.

I am grateful to have met all the stoic, sweet, and brave animals who came through the doors of the ICU. They have
taught me a great deal about dignity. And to their owners who
allowed me to be present in times of joy and also during the
most excruciating moments of sorrow.

Finally, my sincerest thanks to and deepest respect for Dr.
Nishi Dhupa, of the ICU, who patiently and meticulously read
through this manuscript. Nishi was supposed to advise on
medical detail only, but she also caught typos and grammati-

cal gaffes. Her talents are limitless. Nishi is a remarkably gifted veterinarian, not to mention a woman of impressive intellect and true kindness. It is clear to see, as she treats animals, that she has the healing touch.

FOREWORD

by Philip C. Kosch

AS dean of the Tufts University School of Veterinary Medicine, I can count any number of accomplishments we can be proud of here, but placed high among the successes would be our standing in the field of emergency and critical-care medicine. This is one of the newest and fasting-growing segments of veterinary care.

We at Tufts have worked hard to stay out in front. We are leaders in the practice of this highly specialized medicine and in pioneering the training programs for students, interns, and residents. In fact, we are one of only five such formal programs in the United States.

We can boast of a facility that is nothing short of state-of-the-art. Our staff is made up of the specialty's top experts, and we have the cutting-edge technology to speed and sharpen our diagnostics.

Our commitment to emergency and critical care medicine is strong. Clients who come here know their beloved pet will receive the best medical care possible. Veterinarians know they can come here for a superb residency program. That effort has been so successful, in fact, that we have expanded the program—it is now the largest in the country. As part of that expansion, we have developed associations with three other animal hospitals in western Massachusetts, Rhode Island, and Connecticut, and have even acquired an additional emergency practice in our neighboring town of Walpole. These satellite stations allow us to bring our front-line medical care farther out into the community we want to serve.

As a veterinarian, a dean, and a scientist, I'm proud of our leadership in this desperately needed area of animal medicine. But there is so much more to the story.

It was as a client, a man worried about his sick dogs, that I came to truly appreciate the heart of this caring world. During my first year and a half at Tufts, both of my beloved cocker spaniels became ill. They had the best care possible—and I mean that in every sense. In the case of my younger dog, Dr. Susan Cotter turned out to be the world's leading expert on the auto-immune disorder the dog suffered from. Her style, like that of so many others at the hospital, is both caring and very straightforward. It was the worst case she'd seen in her career, and she prepared me for what was to come.

Through four days of transfusions and other treatments, Dr. Cotter and the entire staff supported me emotionally and kept my dog as comfortable as possible. When Daisy died, I received nothing but understanding and kindness.

The older dog, 13, had been battling cancer for quite some time when we arrived here.

Neither dog survived the terrible illnesses that ravaged them, and yet I have no regrets, only appreciation. I know that everything possible was done, and that death for each dog was humane and dignified.

These people who are my staff and colleagues and, more important, members of my community, showed me that being a professional in this realm includes a special knowledge of comfort and care.

The diagnosis may be hopeless, but the humanity is steadfast.

Whether it's the veterinary students, the interns, the residents, or the clinicians, the hospital is a model for compassionate care. At the emergency room, that core value is demonstrated in the most dire of situations.

Owners arrive in panic and distress. And every minute counts. As the dog or cat receives quick response expertise, the owners get a healthy dose of comfort.

The hospital on the campus of a veterinary school is obviously a place of knowledge and science. Our standing in those areas is easy to measure, and we are proud to be leaders. What is harder to measure is something we are just as accomplished in and just as proud of: compassion and understanding.

As you read these pages, you will see that at the Henry and Lois Foster Hospital for Small Animals at Tufts, we know that healing requires both the mind and the heart.

ICU 101

THE drive out through North Grafton, Massachusetts, is spectacular—once past the rows of modern Tudor-style developments, it is pure New
England. Low, mossy stone walls gird hilly pastures. Green
pines dot the corners of the vista, and maples loom large
along the roadway. Cantankerous old farms stand in defiance
of modern times—there's the Nourse Family Farm on the left,
SINCE 1722 reads its understated sign. On the right, black and
white Belted Galloway cows gather. On chill mornings they
stand clustered, shrouded in the mist of their own breath.

No matter the season, the softly rolling fields, dressed in
verdant greens of summer or the yellow ochre of winter, paint
a scene of pastoral perfection. The meandering country road
leads to a hilltop, where the open fields fall away on either
side. Every day, just before sunset, everything here shimmers
in a golden glow.

The soul-quenching beauty of the area, though, is lost on
many of the road's travelers who are headed for The Foster
Hospital for Small Animals. Set on the huge campus of the
Tufts University School of Veterinary Medicine, it is one of

the most sophisticated animal hospitals in the country, and the best hope for beloved pets in an emergency.

Here the cutting-edge field of emergency medicine for animals is pioneering new ground in a state-of-the-art, if cramped, department called the Intensive Care Unit.

Veterinarians travel that bucolic road every day, often before the sun comes up, gulping coffee and blinking themselves awake. They may very well not retrace their steps home till long after the sun has gone down. For patients making the pilgrimage to the ICU, they are likely in a heart-stopping panic to get help. The most they will notice is the DO NOT PASS signs that plague the entire twisted route.

Through the double sets of glass entryway doors is a typical bright waiting room, with the obligatory television set tucked high in a corner. Dogs, cats, birds, rodents, and reptiles wait to see veterinary experts in fields of internal medicine, dentistry, ophthalmology, and oncology.

It's not unusual to see an albino ferret getting an ultrasound, a cat a CAT scan, or a dog hooked up to EKG equipment. One could spy: a water dragon with a tummy ache; an African grey parrot with a prolapsed uterus; a cockatiel who had "aspirated," or breathed in a seed; and a pet rat with a swollen leg, bitten by a guinea pig. The staff of the Intensive Care Unit saves the lives of pets who have sustained the most terrifying traumas, animals who present the most puzzling and dire medical mysteries. Their stomachs have been perforated from swallowed sticks. Their systems are shutting down in shock. Their bones have been crushed by cars. They may be bleeding or choking or collapsing. Brave little animals make their way here, on the threshold of death, and it is up to a team of dedicated emergency vets and staffers to bring them back.

Frightened owners—experiencing what every owner dreads—race here hoping for miracles. Often enough, they get them. They enter the rarefied world of the emergency and critical-care veterinarian. Only three universities in the United States give this training, and Tufts is one of them.

Here, an elite team of doctors are solving cases that few others can. Their realm—the ICU—is truly a world unto itself, with its own rhythms, philosophy, and culture.

The rhythm is nothing less than frenzied. All the time.

The philosophy stems from compassion. That is the core. It colors everything that happens here and stands as a tribute to the bottomless capacity for kindness that some people possess.

The culture? Well, the culture is wild and quirky and intense.

Like any culture, it has its own dress code, diet, language, sense of humor. There's a talk and a walk that is particular to the ICU. Everyone writes notes to themselves on their hands—it's sometimes more convenient than paper. No one ever has scissors when they need them; they've always been left behind somewhere. And when a beeper goes off in a room, everyone looks down automatically at the pagers at their belts. The small cinder-block room of the ICU is lined with double-decker cages, each containing a melancholy fuzzy face. The ICU is crowded with high-tech equipment and high-energy people—three veterinarians are board-certified specialists in emergency and critical care. Under them are eleven residents—fully qualified vets themselves who are seeking to become specialists through a three-year training course. Currently there is one intern, a vet who will spend a year immersed in this kind of medicine. Then there are the fourteen technicians who hold everything together. They draw blood, monitor patients, give medicine (called "meds"), and yes, they clean cages.

The techs have made a fine art of animal care. Once, there was a dalmatian named Dickens who had just come through disc surgery for his troublesome back. He lay on a thick dog bed moaning and crying out. While many would have thought he needed an increase in his pain meds, one of the experienced techs came over and moved him a bit, speaking to him in reassuring tones. "Mostly, these dogs who have had back surgery are not so much in pain as they are anxious about not being able to move quite yet. Sometimes just repositioning a bit and talking to them does the trick." As she readjusted his limp limbs, Dickens relaxed, looking up into her face as she spoke. When she left the run, he closed his eyes and dozed.

The dress code here is simple: wear today what you will still be comfortable in tomorrow, since the shifts tend to spill over into the next day. That means clean blue scrubs; polar tech fleece tops; big, chunky boots.

The diet is simple too. The food is as fast as the pace here: subs, Chinese food, pizza. The residents working around the clock don't require a restaurant to have four stars, only that it own a delivery truck.

The language is interesting, a product of a unique culture.

"What's the best disease we can give him?" doesn't mean "Let's make this dog ill," but, out of all the possible things this dog could have, which would be the best, the most easily treated?

"I just killed her," translates into "I just euthanized that cat."

"Zap some rads," is to take X-rays (as in radiographs).

The extent of bone damage an animal sustains after being hit by a car might be expressed as the level of "crunchiness."

"Ataxic in the hind" means uncoordinated movement of the rear legs. If you hear about a "disease of middle-aged bitches," they are probably talking about something like pyometra, an infection of the uterus that tends to affect older, non-spayed female dogs.

If you want to get fluids into an animal fast, you don't use the slow IV drip, you "bolus" it in—injecting them fast. Suturing an organ in place is to "pexy."

"Icteric" dogs are jaundiced. Like little Brigitte, the cute dachshund whose eyeballs and gums were a strange, sickly yellow. Her red blood cells were being destroyed, probably by an idiopathic immune disorder. *Idiopathic* means of unknown origin, or as one vet says, "idiot medicine, because we don't have an answer."

On the quickie board outside ICU, the day's cases are written in erasable magic marker. The shorthand is in constant use under the complaint section. "HBC" is hit by car. A "down dog" is one that can't get up (a very serious situation). BDLD or "big dog little dog" means a little dog got chewed up by a big one.

At a sophisticated animal hospital such as this, sentiments like "Oh, it's just an animal" are rarely heard. Owners, though, sometimes balk at the estimate for treating pets. "I could buy *four* dogs for that much money," one grumbled. Yet many react like a hardworking owner of a cat with a mysterious, persistent anemia. The projected care could come to $2,000. The owner quietly said, "Oh, my God," but she went forward with treatment nonetheless, no matter the hardship.

Here, veterinarians have completed the same kind of medical training as physicians. All those arduous years of training were endured because of a passion for animals, certainly not for money (the average first-year vet in this kind of environment earns $18,000). Most veterinarians here say they knew all their lives this is what they wanted to do.

Dr. Nishi Dhupa, one of the heads of the ICU, recalls her decision to become a vet. In her soft British accent, the graceful, slight specialist talks about growing up in Nairobi. She was surrounded by the wildlife of Africa, but the culture certainly did not view animals as members of the family. Nevertheless, in the evenings, she would step outside to bid the guard dogs a good night. Once, while hugging one of them tightly, her mother reminded her that she should always love people more than animals. "Not me," she said without hesitation. And her fate was sealed.

Gregarious ICU resident Lisa Powell can also tell you the

exact moment she decided to become a veterinarian. "When I was seven years old, I walked up to my dad after school one day and said, 'Daddy, I want to be an animal doctor.' And I never changed my mind after that."

Dr. Nick Dodman, a Tufts vet and somewhat of a celebrity through his behavior books and TV appearances, didn't always know he wanted to be a vet. But the deep-feeling doctor was aware he was made for medicine. "I loathe suffering," he says. "I still am very upset by any stories of abuse. I've always had this tremendous empathy with people who are suffering and animals who are suffering, and to me it isn't any different." A pivotal moment in his career came when, as he was considering a veterinary education, he went to work for a veterinary practice in Surrey, England. The youngest vet there careened around country roads, traveling from farm to farm in a sleek sportscar. The droll Dodman says, "The turning point, for some curious reason, was that someone wrote in the dust on his car 'Vet 100.' " The ability of this young, hotshot vet impressed Nick. "It was like magic, and I wanted to do that kind of magic too and make the animals well. And it seemed like such a healthy and honorable life."

For resident Ari Jutkowitz, the turning point came with the death of a beloved little parakeet named Charlie. At the time, Ari was six years old, and distraught at the loss of the bird. "In retrospect," he says, "I can figure out exactly what the problem was—he must have had psittacosis [parrot fever], which is common in parakeets. But anyway, from that point on, I was convinced I either wanted to be a pet store owner or a vet." Over time he "realized being a vet was the only way to go."

The clients can be just as committed. Often they have come for a second opinion or a more sophisticated diagnostic test, because their general-practice vets either couldn't decipher the problem or were ill-equipped to treat it. In any event, these people are seeking a higher level of medical care, and have already made an emotional investment to proceed even before they are asked to make a financial one.

The bills can be staggering. People may pay $2,500 for a dog's leg amputation with a follow-up chemotherapy. A dog hit by a car and requiring surgery, a long stay, and perhaps a ventilator can cost $4,000. Some bills have topped $10,000, and few clients carry pet health insurance, though it is available in most states. Out of 120 million pet dogs and cats in the United States, only about 75,000 are covered. With all the sophisticated and costly procedures, owners are increasingly asked to put a price tag on love.

The bond between pets and owners is immeasurable. And there probably is no real comparison—this love stands squarely on its own. The majority of American households— 60 percent—include at least one pet. We'll spend $22 billion on those pets this year alone. We love them like family members, the polls tell us. We carry their photos with us and take them on vacation. When they die, the vast majority of pet owners report, the pain of losing them is as intense as it would be if a close relative had died.

Because of the intensity of that responsibility, the humor in the ICU can be as black and earthy as it is in any place on the front lines of sickness and death and tragedy. Like-minded wits are found among EMTs, cops, journalists, and undertakers.

For example, body fluids can inspire much merriment. When a rabbit urinated voluminously (a bright orange color) onto the white pants of a technician, and in the worst location possible, there were no politely averted eyes. Everyone unmercifully teased the tech about her "accident." Laughing all the way through the telling, exotic animals vet Rose Borkowski, a slim blonde who is normally very quiet, says with delight, "We got a lot of mileage out of that one!"

Scatological humor is abundant. Every year for the holidays, one staffer makes what is known as kitty litter cake.

Though edible, it looks just like a pan of kitty litter, and a couple of Tootsie Rolls are placed on top for good effect. Everyone digs in with relish.

When a collie stood in a caged run that had just been vacated by a diminutive but similar-looking sheltie, someone laughs, "Hey, that dog is half the size he was this morning." Another tech shouts, "Quick! Add water!"

The joking is not always so innocent. One of the most compassionate "softies" of the ICU once walked away from a dead dog everyone had tried to resuscitate for a half hour. "Hope that owner didn't pick up dog food on the way home," she said, to hisses and shocked gasps. It wasn't her patient, and she could distance herself from this one, so she did. In this case, her joke simply said, I've had it with death and dying, and at least one of them isn't going to get to me.

Sometimes one has to wince at the unfortunately named dogs who come in. There's Lexus, who was hit by a car. Streaker had a leg amputated. Lucky was a pup who was first hit by a car and then slated for euthanasia when his owners could not afford his medical expenses. He was lucky enough to be adopted instead of put to sleep, after all.

Indeed, humor is the saving grace, because tragedy can be measured by the number of body bags on the gurney just outside the ICU doors. Some animals simply cannot be saved, like the husky whose entire internal workings were shut down by a massive infection. Some have the potential to be saved, but the owners cannot afford the care, like a Labrador retriever whose bladder was ruptured when he was hit by a snow plow. He had a good prognosis, but the owners could not afford the bill, which would have been at least $800. In other cases, owners give up even when the animal is getting better. One pit bull who had his skull fractured by a car came in with blood dripping from his ear. One eye was rolling around independently of the other, in what is known in medical parlance as *nystagmus* (rapid, involuntary eye movement, which can indicate a problem with the central nervous system). After several days of intensive care, just when his brain swelling was coming down, his owners pulled the plug. They were daunted by the amount of care he may have needed at home.

While the experienced veterinarians have learned to steel themselves (mostly), residents plunge headfirst emotionally into every case. Because they are on the front lines— admitting patients, meeting the owners, and managing the care—the emotions are raw all the time.

Ari Jutkowitz, the twenty-seven-year-old resident who is the dictionary definition of compassion, has his feelings battered during nearly every shift. "I tend to treat emotionally," Ari says. "It seems to me, more emotionally than a lot of the people I see here. I think it gets me into trouble a lot. I latch on to the animal. It's harder to function that way." The slight vet, with wavy dark hair pulled back in a thick ponytail, points out that others are eager at the prospect of solving a tough case, but he sees the agony of a patient before the thrill of medical science. "People who see it as a medical case get interested," Ari says, "but I think, 'Oh, no! Another sick animal, this is really bad.' "

Ari says sometimes he can forget, but not for long. "In the rush of seeing the next case you can kind of turn off what you just saw in your last. But it catches up with you, so that two weeks later, when you have a day off and you're sitting around in your house, something reminds you. And I do get pretty upset by it."

Remembering traumatic cases, Ari gets teary-eyed and his lips tremble. He says, "I'm thinking back to one case in particular, a dog named Apollo. He was a rottweiler. He came in with a mass on his leg and also had some problems with his platelets, and with clotting blood. Probably what's called paraneoplastic syndrome [effects of tumor secretions on some body systems] related to the cancer. His owners were really great people who were trying to accept that their dog needed to have his leg amputated. But then we gave them worse news, that now he's got a clotting problem, and they ultimately decided to put him to sleep. I was pretty upset." It was an older couple, and they wanted to be in the room when Apollo was put to sleep. "I helped them take him out to the car, and I remember the owner saying, 'It's okay, Apollo, we're going home now.' "

Gretchen Schoeffler, another ICU resident, also gets caught up in her cases. Every time the earthy redhead sees a pet, she believes in the animal, falls in love with it, roots for its recovery. After every case she turns to anyone close by and says, as though passing along a confidence, "This is a *really* great dog," or "This is a *really* great cat."

Dr. John Berg is the head of clinical sciences, and the hospital's top surgeon. At the age of forty-four, he is one of the senior staffers. Though this dark-haired vet looks like he should play the romantic lead in a movie, he sees the decrease of emotional involvement as a part of professional maturation.

"The younger the people, the more emotional they're going to get. The more fond they are of the animal, the more upset they get when the animal dies. Have you ever seen any of the doctors, the professional staff, crying over an animal being put to sleep?" he asks. "Not that they don't care, it's just they've gotten past it."

Though the humor is a palliative, what really sustains the vets are the successes. The blue merle collie, in for a toxic reaction to heartworm medication, who bucks the odds and comes back to life after having been resuscitated. (It's estimated that fewer than five percent of animals who need to be resuscitated will ever walk out of an animal hospital.) The Irish setter who battled pneumonia after having a leg amputated and lived to go home, wagging that bright red tail all the way. The cat suffering from complete renal failure who triumphed over one medical hurdle after another. The cat "should have died fifty times" his vet said—but didn't.

The size of the room is tough to work in, but it also leads to an incredible intimacy. All the staffers know about all the cases, even the ones they have nothing to do with. So everyone participates in the emotion. You won't exactly see a group hug, but the humans do often react as one organism.

When Chelsea, a big, sweet St. Bernard, has her X rays clipped up on the light panel, everyone standing around groans in unison. The moth-eaten appearance of one joint indicates osteosarcoma, a painful, tough bone cancer.

But when Rufus, an outgoing yellow lab who was hit by a car and paralyzed in the rear legs, stands up for the first time, it is a big event. "Hey, everyone! Rufus is up!" someone yells, and a cheer goes up in the room. The vets suspected that his spine was just bruised and not permanently damaged, but you can never tell until a moment like this. "It's great to have to tell him to 'stay!'" an ecstatic tech says as she leans over him to adjust his IV line.

As Ari says, to see a healthy patient go home after battling incredible illness is the best feeling in the world.

That's what they fight for. The ICU vets are ace pilots with a top-gun mentality. These vets see the most urgent cases, and often they have only minutes to think it through and act. Hesitation can cost lives. And you can't ask your patient any questions. Their unique combination of encyclopedic medical knowledge, quick reflexes, and confidence saves animals. A certain kind of person is attracted to the ICU.

"Some of it is intellectual," Gretchen explains. "Some of it's the high, the adrenaline rush. I'm a junkie for that. Some of it's probably ego if you're honest with yourself. It's a very powerful position to be in. These are life-and-death situations." Gretchen says so many of these animals are so near death that no one could possibly blame you if lose them. But if you *save* them, you're automatically a hero. "We do lose a lot and that's tough, but when they go home, that makes it all worthwhile."

Lisa Powell thrives on the high-voltage atmosphere. "I like the challenge of an emergency, having [an animal] come to you and you don't know anything that's going on with it. You have this animal lying on the table and you go through your head: what could be going on?" she says. "It's immediate satisfaction. I like wound care and trauma—to me it's challenging. What could be wrong and investigating those things and fixing them."

Much of what these animal doctors do is medical sleuthing. Oftentimes, a dog will have run away and come home sick. Was she hit by a car? Did she eat poison? In one case, a dalmation named Spot was displaying strange neurological signs—shaking and trembling. Given the evidence at hand, the vets wondered whether he had eaten some moldy old meatballs that were tossed out, or if he had been hit by a car and a blood clot migrated to his brain. These are remarkably disparate scenarios, yet each one is a possible fit for what they're seeing. The problem is that each requires a very different course of treatment.

The case load can be overwhelming for the small staff. The residents work grueling shifts, rarely leaving when their actual time is up. The week before Christmas, Gretchen worked a two p.m. to midnight shift, but found herself still treating animals in the ICU at six forty-five the next morning. They are scheduled to work every day for weeks on end, and even when they get a coveted day off, they find themselves coming in to check on a dear patient or to call clients.

The ICU is so captivating, it's almost like a cult. "It's always on my mind. Every day when I wake up, I'm like, 'Hey, I'm going to work today. What about this case or that case?' I think that you get really attached to certain cases. I'm totally involved all the time," Lisa says.

An especially busy time for the ICU is Christmas. Other

vets' offices are closed for the holiday, and the ICU at Tufts is open twenty-four hours a day, 365 days a year. Also, there seem to be more patients in distress.

"How many ways can you make a dog throw up?" Gretchen asks the fourth-year students who are in the current ICU rotation the week before Christmas. Although there is laughter, this is serious holiday planning. With all the chocolate and toxic mistletoe around, plenty of dogs will be heaving their stomach contents out onto the floor of the ICU. The preferred method turns out to be a dose of apomorphine—a morphine derivative—in the eye. This causes an immediate reaction and, just as important, the process can be halted quickly by simply washing out, or *lavaging* the medicine from the eye.

There's another, sadder reason the ICU gets so busy, though. Resident Maureen McMichael says, "In my old practice, they told me that the week before Christmas we euthanize more animals than at any other time during the year. And I thought they were nuts. It didn't make any sense to me. But the logic that they came up with is that people try really hard to hold on to these pets they love through the holidays, but often they finally realize that they just can't, the animal is too ill, and so they all come in, they sort of give up. The week before Christmas in my old practice I once euthanized fifty cases!"

In one sad example, an owner in a red holiday sweater with little embroidered packages on the front learned that her beloved old cat Bobo was dying. The woman visibly crumpled at the news, her tears falling on the festive sweater.

The training, the technology, the expertise, are all comparable to that in a human hospital. But is this like a human hospital? Patients should be so lucky.

When's the last time a physician crawled into bed with a patient and told him in a baby voice how cute he is? When has a nurse rubbed her charges' bellies and sung to them?

The animal ER is a place like no other.

The Case of the Bloated Akita

BY any show standard, Misty is not the best example of an Akita.

Big and bold, members of this Japanese breed were used to hunt bear and boar, and they are meant to have well-defined muscles rippling beneath a lush, dense double coat.

Misty is short. Her coat is skimpy. She's undeniably plump.

On the warm November afternoon she arrived at Tufts, this squat gray dog, who meant more to her owners than all the blue ribbons in the world, was in danger of dying. She was suffering from a gastric emergency that is fairly common but impossible to reverse if not treated quickly. Dog owners rightfully fear this condition and will probably call it "bloat" or "torsion." The veterinary term is *gastric dilatation-volvulus syndrome,* or GDV for short. With GDV, the dog's pouchlike stomach flips over and twists. Medical science is not able to explain why it happens, but it does know which dogs are the most likely candidates: deep-chested dogs such as Irish wolfhounds, standard poodles, German shepherds, Great Danes, and, unfortunately for Misty, Akitas as well.

GDV comes on fast and worsens quickly. Food and water become trapped in the stomach with no escape. The unhappy dog often swallows air, and the stomach becomes distended with gas buildup. The enlarged organ crowds everything around it, including the diaphragm, making breathing difficult and interfering with circulation. The twisted organ tangles blood vessels, and the flow of blood can be cut off to the stomach and the spleen. Blood may pool in the hind end. The blood cannot bring oxygen to these tissues, and cellular waste material accumulates, which is toxic to the system. This kind of circulatory shutdown sends an animal into shock. As a result, many of these dogs die from heart failure.

It's vital to get help as early in the process as possible. The longer the condition is left untreated, and minutes do count, the more likely the tissue of the stomach and spleen will die. Some of this *necrotic* tissue can be surgically removed, though that makes recovery much tougher. Very often there just isn't enough healthy stomach left to save the dog.

Misty's regular vet had already decompressed her stomach, removing gas from the organ with a flexible tube passed down her esophagus. Unable to perform the vital surgery, he had called ahead to alert the hospital of the impending emergency. She was immediately whisked into the ICU on her arrival and tethered to a leg of a stainless steel examining table. Despite pain, anxiety, and the separation from her family, Misty bore all her troubles with a rare dignity.

Too wary and probably uncomfortable to sit or lie down, she stood stoically on the tile floor, quietly observing the whirl of activity around her. And there was plenty to watch.

It was a busy day (there's rarely any other kind) in the ICU. The room is shaped somewhat like a dog's Milk Bone treat. One enters through a wooden door, which opens near the far end. To the immediate right is what looks like a galley kitchen in a Manhattan apartment. The refrigerator holds medicines, blood products, and cat and dog food. There is also an oddity here—a flushing sink. Gadgets that may at first glance look like a microwave and a food processor are actually high-tech centrifuges and blood-testing equipment. To the immediate left, a long, narrow desk area hugs the back wall. The section is crowded with knapsacks and lunch bags underneath, and papers and well-worn reference books on top. Large plastic mugs of coffee are perched precariously on many different surfaces.

In front of the desk is a narrow band of floor space and a long row of double-tiered cages, forming the long portion of the room. At the end of this row, where the room comes out to the other T, are two stainless steel examining tables in the center, with three "runs" for large dogs on one side and a double oxygen chamber on the other. Incubators that fit cats or small dogs are tucked in at various corners. Electric shavers hang from the ceiling (fur is shaved off for IV lines, belly taps, and other procedures). Electronic IV delivery systems—blue plastic boxes with digital readouts—stand outside each cage with flexible tubing feeding in and out. Crash carts, drawers of equipment, trash cans, mops, and buckets add to the crush and chaos. Technicians, students, residents, and specialists dance around one another as though they've all been well choreographed.

On the afternoon Misty came to the ICU, every cage and run was full, with four more dogs on gurneys cramping the already tight space. There were emergencies everywhere: a five-year-old greyhound who had been hit in the leg with a crowbar; a very unhappy dalmatian who'd had disc surgery and was barking and howling with anxiety; a Gordon setter recovering from abdominal surgery; a golden retriever hit by a car eight days before and experiencing what appeared to be a mysterious medical relapse of some kind; and a Great Pyrenees on a mat on the floor attached to an IV drip. The constant din of a ringing phone adds to the pandemonium.

This is what Misty faces. Even on a happy day, Akitas wear what looks like a worried expression—wrinkled forehead over tiny eyes—and in this strange medical environment, Misty seems rightly concerned. She stands solidly, feet planted firmly. Only her dark face reveals her quiet anxiety.

As with human hospitals, emergencies are prioritized in the triage system—the most severely compromised patients get attention first. A technician or vet student usually goes out to the waiting room to make this determination. A fourth-year vet student does a preliminary examination and reports the findings to the resident in charge of the case. Because Misty's vet had already called in, and it was known in advance that she was a high priority, she was led back to ICU quickly.

Both the student and the resident go over the dog's medical history. It is a vital step in the care of any animal. The mention of little odd details can end up saving a life. For example, one owner said as an afterthought that his sick dog had possibly gotten into some old meatballs. Moldy food can be highly toxic and even cause neurological damage. Another owner mentioned in passing that her sick cat kept getting her nails caught on the rug. Fast nail growth can signal thyroid problems.

Ari says, "Something that I was taught in school is: Always let the client tell their story. No matter what you do, they're not going to be happy until they've said what's bothering them. And you always have to address their concerns. Something may sound trivial to you, but it's not trivial to them."

Dr. John MacGregor is the intern who takes over Misty's case. Though he is a quiet man, his height, square shoulders, and red hair give him immediate presence. Wearing blue hospital scrubs and a white lab coat, he meets Misty's owners, Cheryl and David Alger, in one of the many small examining rooms. The distraught husband and wife sit on a low visitors bench. Testifying to the sudden nature of GDV, David, a Master Class competitive cyclist, is still wearing black spandex pants and black polar fleece pullover from a training run he had just completed when Misty got sick. In the car, they had reached speeds of ninety-five miles an hour trying to get her here.

They tell John that the dog had been outside for about ten minutes when David returned home to find her salivating excessively and dry heaving—retching without producing anything. Knowing a great deal about the breed, they had recognized immediately what Misty's problem was.

"We always thought we'd lose her to bloat," Cheryl says.

"We didn't think we'd have her long," David agrees.

And then Cheryl says softly, "We have that kind of luck."

John leans across the stainless steel examining table, elbows down on the wide surface, and listens as the Algers recall Misty's symptoms and the time it started. Then John explains the situation. Though the Algers already understand that Misty has GDV, and though they know a great deal about the condition, it's important for John to give a quick overview to be sure. He also tells them that back in ICU, he was able to pass a tube into Misty's stomach to relieve the pressure until the surgeon arrives.

John says there's no way to tell if the stomach and spleen have been damaged until they operate. It is a very serious procedure, and there are dangers to worry about during surgery and many possible complications afterward.

John pauses. The part of the talk that all the vets hate to give is the next one, regarding money. Typically, the cost of such surgery and post-op care is $2,000 to $2,200, and half is required up front as a deposit. John's tone is apologetic. He also has to add, "For some reason, Akitas tend not to do as well as others with this. The cost could end up significantly higher."

Standing in the emergency examining room, residents must outline dire circumstances and big bills time after time. They never know how owners will react. Some show anger. A few display nonchalance. Most react with sorrow and tears.

The financial question complicates everything, since few owners carry pet health insurance. It's hard to judge who will go forward with medical care and who won't. Some wealthy clients don't think it's worth the money. Some poor clients spend everything and go into debt. On many occasions veterinarians have the ability to save a beloved pet, but the traumatized owners simply cannot gather the resources to pay for the care. So whenever an estimate is given, there is some anxiety in the seconds or minutes of silence that follow.

Cheryl looks John in the eye and says, "We love her to pieces." David adds, "She's like a member of the family." Some days, statements like those are followed by a "but." Not today. The Algers came here to save their dog, no matter what the cost.

Then Cheryl remembers an important detail. She tells John of another complicating factor, that Misty has had trouble tolerating anesthesia before. John makes a note.

Cheryl begins to outline Misty's medical history—some thyroid problems and bouts of bladder infections—and through it the dog's life story comes out. The Algers adopted Misty two years ago. They had done eighteen months' worth of research to select a breed that would suit them. Cheryl wanted a big dog, and they needed one who would be quiet and content while the couple was gone at work. Akitas, they discovered, are notorious couch potatoes.

Both the high cost of an Akita and the fact that they lived in a condo made them hesitate. But then fate stepped in, when Cheryl got a call from the local dog officer. She had an Akita, but, Cheryl was warned, this girl had been through a lot. Used by a puppy mill breeder who mated Misty repeatedly to churn out high-price pups, Misty had been poorly cared for, exploited, probably abused, and when her reproductive abilities had slowed, she was tossed out on the street to fend for herself. Misty's intelligence, her watchful nature, and her ability to blend into the background helped her survive the next month of scavenging and hunting till she was caught by animal control.

When the Algers saw Misty, she was an emaciated sixty pounds, what little coat she had was matted, and that signature curled Akita tail was bald, Cheryl says, "like an opossum's." Her eyelids were malformed, flipped outward and exposing the moist red mucous membrane tissue. She had just been spayed and was very sick. Cheryl says she looked like "a dilapidated old house."

Cheryl "fell in love with her right away," but as so often happens, Misty fell in love with someone else. Cheryl says, "The minute we got her home, she was David's dog."

Having been deprived of a normal life, she was, Cheryl says, "an animal who had never learned even to play with a ball."

The Algers lavished her with affection, giving her morning medications disguised in cream cheese, doting on her, applying daily ointment to her tender eyelids. Experimenting with all kinds of specialty foods, they finally cleared up her skin rashes by feeding her a canned-fish and potatoes diet. They patiently drew her out. They discovered her weakness for ice cubes and the doggie ice cream substitute, Frosty Paws.

Things were going so well, they decided to gamble. They bought another, younger Akita, hoping Misty would love the companionship, but fearing she might withdraw further into herself.

"She just blossomed," Cheryl says, smiling. Patches, a pinto Akita, made Misty happy. Misty is still very mellow and laid-back, the Algers say, but she is content. That is expressed in her bearing, which they quite accurately describe as "regal."

Having given the green light to surgery, the Algers ask John if they can come back to the ICU to say good-bye to their girl, knowing it could be the last time they see her alive. If the surgeon opens up Misty and finds extensive damage to the stomach, John will call them with that update. Given the level of risk with the surgery, and the potential for a long and expensive hospital stay, many owners opt at that point for their pets to be put to sleep on the table. Surgical resident Caroline Garzotto, who will be performing Misty's surgery, has seen these bills spiral to $10,000. And there's no guarantee the dog will go home.

The worried look Misty has worn vanishes as Cheryl and David approach her. They whisper to her and pat her for a few moments and walk away. Misty cries out in frustration as they leave, and Cheryl can't fight back tears as she heads for the front desk.

The Algers are hardly alone in their devotion to their dog. As a *Newsweek* magazine article pointed out, "The advent of high-tech pet medicine underscores a deep change in the way people regard their animals." The magazine went on to state, "America's 117 million dogs and cats receive better care than many of its citizens."

Animals receive pacemakers and organ transplants. They undergo hip-replacement surgery. Veterinary oncologists, ophthalmologists, and dentists provide chemotherapy, radiation, laser treatments for cataracts, and root canals.

Polls and surveys have revealed over the years that pets are solid members of the family. Seventy-nine percent of us take them on vacation. We sleep with them in our beds. We carry pictures of them in our wallets. A study by the Waltham pet food company in 1996 revealed that 100 percent of pet owners talk to their pets; 97 percent feel the animals know what they are saying. And 78 percent speak for their pets, imagining what they would say if they could talk.

Nearly half the respondents to a Pfizer/Gallup Organization poll said they would spend thousands to care for a seriously ill or injured dog, even if that meant borrowing money to do so. Three out of five owners in that same survey said their dogs were among the most important things in their lives. The majority of people went so far as to say that in certain respects, dogs are better companions than some family members.

According to a 1998 survey by the American Animal Hospital Association, an amazing 83 percent of pet owners said that they were likely to risk their own life for their pet.

Though there has been a profound shift in the way we think about our pets, it's a love affair that has been going on for a long time. A huge dog cemetery from the fifth century B.C. has been unearthed in Israel at Ashkelon. According to *National Geographic* magazine, "Each dog—from puppies to elderly adults—was carefully placed on its side in a shallow pit, legs flexed." At another archaeological dig in the Upper Jordan Valley, the remains of an elderly person clutching a puppy were discovered in a burial site dated to 12,000 years ago.

Today, we are still puzzling out this mysterious bond.

A study from the State University of New York at Buffalo Medical School suggests that dogs will be of more comfort to people in a stressful situation than their spouses. One hundred twenty men and women were given a stressful task to perform—making a speech, solving a mathematical problem, or dipping a hand in cold water. Subjects were accompanied by either their spouse, a friend, or their dog. Their heart rates and blood pressure were monitored. The result? They were most stressed out with their spouses, and most relaxed with their dogs.

Study after study over the last decade has shown how good for people pets are. In an increasingly withdrawn world, dogs facilitate social interactions. People who are seriously ill report that their dogs distract them from their pain. Because dogs need to be walked, owners are often in better shape. Just petting our dogs lowers our blood pressure (and, interestingly, the dog's, too). The blood pressure of children drops if a dog so much as enters a room. And heart-attack victims with pets show a higher one-year survival rate.

If a pill had this many beneficial effects, a researcher once said, you could bottle it and become a multimillionaire.

Great writers from Lord Byron to Elizabeth Barrett Browning to John Steinbeck have written lovingly of their pets. In O'Neill's "The Last Will and Testament of an Extremely Distinguished Dog," he writes in the voice of his departed dalmatian Blemie: "No matter how deep my sleep I shall hear you, and not all the power of death can keep my spirit from wagging a grateful tail."

According to James Serpell, associate professor of humane ethics and animal welfare at the School of Veterinary Medicine, University of Pennsylvania, the reason we have so much trouble creating an accurate vocabulary for the relationship between humans and pets is that—believe it or not—this interaction is still mysterious even to those who investigate it. Science hasn't yet identified the mechanism by which dogs and other pets appear to have such a clear-cut psychological and physiological benefit.

Part of it is uncritical and uncompromising love. "People search their whole lives for unconditional love," psychologist Sharyn Rose of Framingham, Massachusetts, says, "and we find it in our pets."

When lives hang in the balance in a veterinary emergency room, emotions run high. An hour after the Algers leave Misty, the dog is in the operating room. Caroline Garzotto, thirty-four, a surgical resident in the second year of a three-year term and the weekend surgeon on call, has studied the case file and is ready to go.

Misty is lying on the table, belly up. Her mouth is ajar, and her tongue hangs out sidesaddle around a breathing tube attached to a ventilator. Her belly has been shaved, scrubbed with several antibiotic solutions, and coated in orange iodine. Unconscious, Misty is covered, head to toe, with blue paper, opened only at her abdomen.

As is often the case, the entire team—one student to administer anesthesia and monitor the ventilator, two to assist the surgeon—is made up of women.

Entering the operating room, Caroline gets right to work. She makes an incision straight down Misty's bare abdomen, and a student uses a cauterizing pen to seal off the little blood vessels along the incision.

"These cases are either very straightforward, with things already back in place," Caroline says through her paper surgical mask, "or the stomach is still twisted, which can be very bad, or the spleen might have to come out."

She uses the blade to cut through a layer of fat, and poor Misty has plenty of it. The student removes some fat (a canine tummy tuck?) so Caroline can see in. Metal braces hold the incision open. Caroline surveys the scene before doing anything else. Long ago, augers would foretell the future by examining the entrails of animals. At this moment Caroline examines Misty's insides to see if the dog will even have a future.

Everyone in the room is rooting for Misty, and there's tension as Caroline begins to announce what she sees in her explorations. She's giving play-by-play to an eager group.

"Liver looks okay."

There is the wet sound of organs being moved.

"Spleen looks good!"

"Stomach looks good."

A feeling of relief fills the room. Caroline unkinks the organ and points to a red, inflamed area of tissue where the esophagus meets the stomach. The twist has clearly irritated this section, but Caroline says the redness is fine. When this tissue has turned purple or black, it's bad news. Surgical masks and head coverings obscure the better part of all the faces in the room, but eyes shine and smiles are obvious all around.

"This is the best-case scenario," Caroline proclaims. "If we had had to resect, her chances would have gone down by fifty percent." That's most likely due to the animal being in shock longer and the prolonged time anesthesia had to be administered.

This is what Caroline loves about being a surgeon. "I like to do things with my hands and to be more active. And I like to see an immediate result. Plan a procedure, execute it, and then you see the results. You get that satisfaction out of it. Which is part of why surgeons hate it when things go bad. We expect everyone to get better after surgery."

Bloat cases can easily go either way. "You're always holding your breath until you open it up and look at the stomach and see: Is it still viable? Is it ruptured?" If more than half of the stomach is dead, she is faced with either having to resect it, or simply to put the dog to sleep on the table. "Fifty percent of those dogs may die just from going through the shock of the whole thing, losing half their stomach. The resection can be difficult if the damage to the stomach is up near the esophagus because it's really hard to close those areas."

If the blood supply has been cut off to the spleen for a long time, that may have to go, too, though this is not as risky as losing part of the stomach. Also, as Caroline notes, the dogs can still die after the operation or be in the hospital longer.

"There's always a sigh," Caroline says, when the organs in a bloat case look fine. "You say, 'Thank God,' when there doesn't have to be a resection—those can be pretty rough if it's really bad in there."

Another tube is passed down Misty's throat to get rid of any remaining gas. Caroline points out a spot where the rhythmic motion of the stomach tissue can be clearly seen—Misty's peristalic action is working well, constricting and contracting in the normal flow to move things along the digestive tract. The surgeon decides to perform *gastropexy*, or attach Misty's stomach to the abdominal wall to prevent another incident like this. Two layers of stomach and two layers of the wall are cut open and sutured together in what Caroline describes as "kissing style."

Next, the area is flushed in saline solution poured from a little kidney-shaped plastic tub. Then the team can close. "Every time you look at it, it looks better and better," Caroline says happily as she examines the healthy organs inside Misty's belly.

One of the concerns with these cases, Caroline explains, is that you can have problems with the heart. Sometimes as the stomach is untwisted, tissues that have been deprived of oxygen release "a cascade of free radicals," resulting in heart dysrhythmias. Also, toxins from the intestines can harm the heart.

But not this time. Misty's surgery has gone well, and her anesthesia has been smooth. Extensive suturing—on three layers—plus surgical staples at the end seal the dog back up.

Alison Hayward, a tall, striking vet student with a British accent and shoulder-length hair who has been handling Misty's anesthesia, smiles and leans in to Misty's furry face. "You lucked out big-time, doll."

Everyone laughs because it's so true.

As the anesthesia is stopped, Caroline says, "I have a feeling she's going to spring right up." Sure enough, before the gurney is spun out of the operating room, Misty awakens with a soft moan. The dog who likes to be in control struggles to clear her head.

At six-fifteen, the awakening dog is tucked into a small, bottom-tier cage. A little foam bed and blankets make her recovery space look cozy. While other dogs bark in cages all around her, Misty regains consciousness in this strange place and makes not a sound.

*   *   *

The next day, Sunday, is another heavy-duty shift in the ICU. If there is a theme today, it is fluids. A technician has quickly pulled a heavy, soaking wet dog bed from an upper cage, accidently spraying everyone with urine. Urine from several cages is being squeegeed into the floor drains. Plus, a bucket filled with the blood of a dog suffering from internal bleeding has been knocked off a high examining table, splashing everyone within a five-foot radius and giving the area all around the look of a crime scene.

Misty is now awake in her cage, looking drowsy and placid. Her bearing throughout her medical ordeal has been unchanged. She seems to maintain a serene distance from all she is being put through. But she doesn't miss a beat.

At 2:25, something wonderful happens to Misty—her owner visits. Cheryl and her mother, Alice, sit in an examining room waiting for Misty. As the dog enters the room, she cannot contain her joy. Despite the painful surgery she has just endured, she runs to Cheryl, vocalizing in a soft cry. Misty sits before Cheryl and places both front paws up on her chest. She looks Cheryl in the eyes and cries insistently as though trying to tell her all that's happened.

Cheryl laughs as she hugs and strokes the dog. "That's Akita talk," she explains. They visit for a while, but Misty is obviously uncomfortable. She has not urinated in her cage and, being a dutiful, house-trained dog, she won't go here in this room, either. She's been holding it for quite some time, determined to maintain her canine etiquette and not have an accident indoors. The ICU technician suggests that Cheryl take Misty out to relieve herself, but Cheryl is afraid Misty will be too excited at the thought of going home. She'll be terribly disappointed when she has to come back in. So the technician will take her. But as much as Misty has to go to the bathroom, she is reluctant to leave her owner and go out with a stranger.

"I can't protect you this time, kid," Cheryl says to her. Misty disappears down the hallway, led by a technician on the other end of a small blue leash.

Misty will get to go home the next day. Despite the final bill of $1,400, her owners feel richer to have their dear dog back.

SHOCK

GEORGE and Melody LeFrancois are in the middle of a dog owner's worst nightmare. At nine o'clock on a crisp, bright Thursday in December, they roar into the hospital parking lot. Melody is sobbing and George, at the wheel, struggles to hold himself together through the crisis.

Their beloved three-legged husky, Meka, is lying on the backseat, vomiting blood and barely able to breathe. Back at home, the lifeless body of their other, older husky, Wolfie, lies on the garage floor, his backyard grave only half dug in the frozen earth and hastily abandoned.

A fast-moving mystery ailment, like something out of a movie, is to blame. Whatever it is that killed Wolfie is now ravaging his young and strong companion. Their local vet could not help, so the couple is racing against time to get Meka the most sophisticated care possible. The twenty-five-minute ride has been agonizing, as Melody watched Meka's blue eyes fixed in a blank stare. With no ambulances for pets, George gripped the wheel and dealt with the frustration, over and over again, of being stuck behind slow-moving cars on the winding segment of Route 30 leading to the hospital. There was no way to signal the morning commuters that behind them a life was being lost.

Finally they arrive. Melody is overcome with emotion. As George checks in at the desk, a researcher from the behavior clinic who happens to be passing through takes Melody to the rest room so she can put a cold cloth on her face and collect herself. A technician from the Intensive Care Unit hurries to see Meka. Under the triage system, in which the worst cases are seen first, Meka becomes the ICU's top priority.

Meka's frightening condition mobilizes the ICU into action. Everyone begins to move in the cramped quarters like a medical drill team. Dr. Lisa Powell, a thirty-one-year-old resident, in chinos and a blue T-shirt, takes charge. All eyes are on the young vet with the cascading, curly dark hair. In the past, she has been overheard grumbling, "I can't stand it when they ask me, 'How long have you been a vet?' " Because she looks so young and has such a ready sense of humor, one might be fooled into thinking she is younger than she really is, or less serious about her work. But in a crisis she is transformed; intense and decisive, she swings into action.

The dog is in shock, so Lisa immediately orders IV fluids and oxygen. When an animal is in shock, blood flow is reduced, and vital oxygen and nutrients do not reach tissue, causing organs to shut down. Meka's condition is probably the result of some infectious problem, so everyone must wear gloves and everything the dog touches must be bleached.

Valerie Kouloyan, the head technician, and her assistant Matt work together to shave through the husky's thick black fur and place an IV catheter in her neck. Blood is drawn from a back leg, and with analyzing equipment right in the ICU, it only takes minutes for important information to be revealed. In the interim, fluids are started and Lisa lifts the dog's lips to check her gums. The color of the gums, ranging from pale to brick red or almost purple, tells doctors a great deal about a patient's condition. Pressing on the gums and watching the color change indicates *capillary refill time*, or how quickly blood flow is operating. Meka's gums are a dark, angry red.

Lisa orders a group of blood tests called "the big four": a hematocrit, which determines the red-blood cell volume; the total solids, or blood proteins; blood glucose, which reveals blood-sugar levels; and blood-urea nitrogen, an indicator of kidney function. The total solids count is high: Meka is very dehydrated. Her hematocrit is high and her blood glucose is low. Her blood pressure is dangerously low, 61 over 28. Normal is 110 to 180 over 60 to 100. The blood work plus new details about what has happened to her indicate she is in what's called "septic shock," a deadly condition that kills as many as 80 percent of its victims. Lisa's plan is to get Meka stabilized as quickly as possible. That means IV fluids and oxygen to begin with. Antibiotics and a blood transfusion will follow.

In an examining room close to the ICU, Melody and George begin to relax a bit, knowing Meka now has expert care. Melody, still teary, tells their story.

The young couple were famous in their hometown for their two huskies. Both dogs had been rescued, probably from abuse, and, amazingly, both had had front legs amputated before finding a home with the LeFrancoises. Wolfie was an older, more refined dog, the kind whose eyes were windows to his soul. When George found him years before, the husky was roaming the streets, a sorry character with matted, filthy fur, hobbling about scrounging for food. Something about him made George stop his truck. He opened the passenger-side door and looked down at the flea-bitten stray. Kiddingly, George challenged the three-legged dog. "Okay, if you can get yourself up in the cab of this truck, I'll take you home." Wolfie did it. George, a man of his word, took the dog home, and then immediately to a grooming salon. Melody, who is as blue-eyed as her huskies, looks up. "You would not believe how beautiful he was after that bath!" His bushy coat, lupine ears, and sharp muzzle earned him the name Wolfie.

The fell in love with the dog—he was such a good boy as they ran their business, a seasonal seafood shack in Mendon, Massachusetts. Just as they began to think about getting a friend for Wolfie, they saw a curious ad in the newspaper. Another three-legged husky was in need of a home.

Enter Meka.

She had been found tied up at a playground, her left front leg dangling after probably being hit by a car. When the two dogs met, Wolfie reclined at Meka's feet. "We got her as a friend to Wolfie three and a half years ago," George says, smiling, "but she was really more of a menace. We always say, 'Meka is the dog. Wolfie is the son.'" Their restaurant, the Redwood, became known as "the place with the wolves." The fencing company they hired even came up with the idea of building a petting window into the gate so enthusiastic diners could say hello to the popular dogs. The funniest thing the LeFrancoises heard, and heard frequently, was the question: Had the two dogs been Siamese twins who were separated at the leg? Sitting in the cinder-block examining room, as distraught as they are, George and Melody have to laugh at the notion still.

They were a young, happy couple, with two healthy dogs and a thriving business. Life was good. But a bizarre disease has changed all that. Something that seemed harmless has set off a deadly chain of events. By talking to George and Melody, the medical staff feel they knew what the culprit was in this medical mystery.

Since the restaurant was shut down for the winter, everyone was home over the last several days. Wolfie, out in the backyard, discovered a long-buried rawhide bone. It might have been repugnant to look at, but the dog relished the filthy, mangled chew toy. Looking out the window, Melody saw what was going on, but resisted the temptation to take the treat away. Meka joined in and chewed some, too. At the time, Melody didn't think twice about it.

Soon after, Wolfie fell horribly ill. He began vomiting and had diarrhea. That rawhide bone was probably buried while still moist, and it became loaded with bacteria in the soil. Their regular veterinarian put Wolfie on IV fluids for an entire day, but told the LeFrancoises they could take him home overnight, as no one would be staffing the clinic and Wolfie would surely be more comfortable at home. They all knew the poor dog was gravely ill, and the plan was to treat him again first thing the next morning.

Worried about him, Melody checked on Wolfie repeatedly throughout the night. At 5:00 A.M., while it was still dark, Melody tiptoed out of bed and found her dear old dog without any life left in him. He was gone. She and George cried over Wolfie and then set about the hard task of digging a grave for him. They wanted him, even in death, to be close to them. Melody remembers watching traffic pass by their house and thinking about how routine life was for everyone out there, while her world had just changed so tragically.

There would be no time for contemplation, though. As George was shoveling the hard earth for Wolfie, Meka began to vomit. She was losing control of her bodily functions just as Wolfie had.

They hurried Meka to the clinic and were told the dog's only chance for survival would be at Tufts, the closest animal hospital.

Now, inside the ICU, Lisa Powell has a very sick dog on her hands.

Dr. Nishi Dhupa is an expert among experts in the ICU. Double-boarded in both internal medicine and emergency medicine, she is a skilled veterinarian and a calm presence. She quickly sizes up how dire this situation is. She's seen many dogs in septic shock. "It's very typical that the ones in an advanced stage fail because they've been so deprived of oxygen for a certain amount of time. The ones that are not so advanced you probably can resuscitate—they may be okay, and they may stay okay. The ones that fail are the ones that you know are really far gone already. Then the prognosis becomes much worse immediately.

"Some of them are just not going to keep the heart going. If you get to that point, you know that you've got a less than one percent chance of bringing them back."

Meka's prognosis is so dire, Lisa can't afford a misstep. She needs a blood culture, which must be "a sterile stick," so Matt begins to shave Meka's rear right leg. It is 10:25. Lisa leaves the room to check on another patient, a diabetic cat also in dire circumstances. While the electric clippers buzz, Meka struggles to stay alert, but her eyes roll back in her head. Seconds later, she suddenly rouses. She begins to cough and then vomit. Bright red blood pours from the sick animal's mouth. "Page Dr. Powell, stat!" Matt yells.

Matt is a tall, muscular man, towering over everyone else in ICU, and he invariably is asked to do the heavy lifting. There is no need to ask this time. He sweeps the limp dog up in his arms and carries her to a stainless steel examining table. An ICU vet and a resident drop everything and come over. Val is suddenly there, too. Meka seems more alert after the episode; she is licking her lips and looking around. Val strokes her head.

Within seconds Lisa Powell is back in the ICU with her patient. "Oh, honey," she says soothingly, "don't die. What are you doing, you good girl, scaring us like that?" She turns to the team. "She got glucose too fast. It shouldn't have been bolused." Medications and fluids can be infused slowly, through an IV catheter, or they can be bolused, meaning injected quickly. With a dog in Meka's condition, the desire is to get as much help into her as fast as possible, but her body can't necessarily handle it all.

Nonetheless, once again Meka appears better. It is 10:35.

Val finishes the task of shaving Meka's rear leg and scrubs

the skin down with gauze soaked in a bright red solution, Nolvasan. Next, the area is cleaned with gauze saturated with alcohol. There is a great deal of tension in the room. The usual banter is gone. Val solemnly continues her work.

Moments later, Meka lifts her head ever so slightly from the table and begins to howl weakly. Her cry is long, sustained, and otherworldly. She does seem like a wolf now, this big black dog with a delicate white blaze running from her nose to her forehead. As she moans her wild, mournful call, her small white eyebrows knit together in concentration. She has lost her male companion and now she, too, is facing death.

At 10:42, Valerie slowly draws blood into a syringe from Meka's back leg. Minutes later, a vet student checks her heartbeat and takes a rectal temperature. It is 102.5—within normal range. But it's the only bit of good news and even that may not last. A fever could be on the way. Information about the blood tests comes in. Meka's white blood cell count is 480; normal if 6,000. Her platelet count of 2,000 should be more like 200,000. The total solids reading is 1.4—normal would be 7.0. Worst of all, she has zero neutrophils, a blood component needed to fight off invading microorganisms.

"Bad, bad, bad," Lisa says softly as she hears the news. "Dang it!" She gives herself a second to absorb the information and then puts her hands on her hips. "All right." Lisa concentrates and then does something characteristic—she turns to the dog. "Awww, honey." Later, Lisa will explain that other people may not appreciate the pain of animals, but she does. In these situations she always remembers to comfort as well as treat.

"To me, you have to be so much more kind and compassionate with animals. When you have a really hurt person, you have so many people that are compassionate and empathetic and sympathetic." Yet, she says, "when you have an animal that's sick, a lot of people think, 'Oh, it's just an animal.'

"I remember this African grey parrot that lived at the clinic I worked at when I was seventeen. Her name was Pita Marie, and she was awesome. And she only liked certain people for some reason. She liked me and we got along. I taught her how to play dead." When Lisa was at school as an undergraduate, the clinic called her one day to say that Pita had died from a fungal infection in her lungs. "I wasn't there and my roommate took the call. When I got home, she said, 'They called you from the clinic. They told me not to tell you what happened, but I asked them anyway, and I told them I'd just tell you. You know, some bird died.'" At first Lisa was in shock. Her whole body froze. Then all her emotions came pouring out. "I called up and I'm crying on the phone and I'm grabbing all my pictures of her that I have. It was disastrous, and I just remember my roommate saying, 'You're so weird. It's just a bird.'"

But it wasn't just a bird. Lisa had bonded with Pita Marie, and she was a close friend to her.

"So I think that when it comes to animals, they need more compassion. They can't talk to you. They can't tell you things. They don't understand when they're sick. And I think the owners too, who care so much about them, don't necessarily get much support. If I said, 'My mother died,' everybody would be saying, 'Oh, no.'" On the other hand, "if I said, 'My dog died,' they'd say, 'Oh sorry, why don't you get another one?'"

Lisa feels that talking to these frightened animals is vital. "I think that's a part of healing. I think that they know. They're in a strange place, they're sick, they don't know what's going on. They don't know you're trying to help them. They've got needles in them. Somebody keeps coming around every two hours, sticking them with stuff, and they're thinking, 'What the heck is going on? I'm used to wrapping up in my owner's bed and being warm and cuddly and getting hugs and kisses. So what is this?'"

Meka may be too far gone even to hear the kind words spoken to her.

Treatment in this case is an uphill battle. The word goes out—no white blood cells in the patient means she's very vulnerable to any infection. Everything has to be extremely sterile, and it's important to minimize who has contact with her. One or two techs will be assigned to Meka.

Lisa paints a dark picture: The blood counts, particularly the zero neutrophils, are actually "incompatible with life." Somehow, Meka is still alive, running on her own strong spirit and the science of the ICU staff.

One thing's for sure—with a raging infection like this, it's time to bring out the broad spectrum, or "big gun" antibiotics: Baytril, Metronidazole, Cefazoline. Cimetidine is given to protect the stomach.

Everything is being done for the dog, but later Lisa will reflect:

"I think that I knew that she might not make it. I was hoping, though, because she came in pretty sick, but then we got her going pretty well. She seemed stable and then . . ." Her voice trails off. "But that's the problem with sepsis—at any second their organs fail again and they go into DIC [disseminated intravascular coagulation, in which the clotting system fails, creating clots everywhere] or they start bleeding a lot, or the infection causes the heart to not work very well."

But they keep trying. Still on the examining table, Meka receives more fluids and antibiotics. As Val works on the many fluid lines, Meka once again goes rigid, extending her head out and stretching her neck. These are agonal breaths—a last-ditch effort on the body's part to take in some oxygen and to stay alive.

Under normal circumstances, blood to be transfused into a dog is warmed up, but Lisa says in this case there is no time. "We need it stat!"

The student who is setting up an oxygen line fumbles, and

Lisa rushes past him. Plugging in the line on an adjacent examining table, she gently places the oxygen mask over Meka's nose. Again, the crisis passes. Meka is stabilized enough to be moved into an ICU cage lined with blankets. It is 11:10.

Lisa is kneeling on the floor holding the oxygen mask over Meka's muzzle when Val arrives with the blood.

Nishi discusses the case with Lisa. The presence of toxic changes in the neutrophils points toward a gram-negative infection. It looks like a virulent strain of salmonella is to blame, and on top of that, Meka may be suffering from pneumonia as well, probably as a result of aspirating some vomit. This is a fairly common phenomenon in cases like this.

All the medical evidence is pointing in the same direction, and a urine culture to detect bacteria is ordered. Medications arrive from the in-hospital pharmacy, and they are injected into the neck catheter and into the fluid bags.

Blood pressure is still low, 70 over 47, and Lisa wonders aloud about ordering Dopamine, which would help raise Meka's blood pressure. Pulse oxygen level is "terrible, but better than it was." At 11:30, a bag of 6 percent Hetastarch in 0.9 percent sodium chloride injection is started.

But Meka takes a turn for the worse. Her jaw opens and her jerky breathing movements mean she has begun agonal breathing again.

Once more she is raced to an examining table. Val and Matt, along with ICU vets Gretchen Schoeffler, Liz Rozanski, and Nishi Dhupa, join Lisa on the case.

Val squeezes a breathing bag or "ambu." Liz Rozanski checks the EKG. Gretchen Schoeffler hunts down a ventilator. Matt syringes 30 ccs of sodium chloride solution into the blood bag. Lisa, now stained with Meka's blood, leaps up onto a high examining table to connect a suction tube. Everyone is working together.

Plasma arrives, and Liz announces that Meka is once again

breathing on her own, though she is being "peeped" or occasionally assisted. (PEEP stands for "positive end–expiratory pressure.)

A rectal temp is taken, and the thermometer comes out coated in blood. She is bleeding everywhere. Gretchen brings in a big, fluffy mustard-colored blanket, and Meka is lifted while it is placed on the table.

Despite the heroic efforts, by 12:05 Meka is going downhill. She vomits pure blood, which collects in a puddle below the examining table. Nothing seems to be stopping the raging infection, and her entire body is shutting down.

Gretchen says that Meka's heartbeat is "pretty good," but her whole back end is rigid. She's dying, a little bit at a time.

Within ten minutes, Meka is losing consciousness. Lisa holds her head up and calls her name. "Meka? Meka?" She says out loud what she hasn't wanted to believe all along. Meka has less than a five percent chance of making it.

The dog is suffering and to go full bore in treatment now—letting a ventilator do the breathing—would most likely prolong the agony. The LeFrancoises could easily run up a tab of $4,000 (due in large part to the expensive use of the ventilator, which requires constant monitoring) and still not take their dog home. They are summoned to make a decision.

The emotional upheaval in the tiny ICU is almost unbearable.

Melody, physically and emotionally exhausted from the sleepless night, is sobbing Meka's name.

The busy ICU comes to an absolute standstill. Everyone is solemn. Some are also crying where they stand.

"I can't kill her," Melody sobs. Her husband, George, holds her. He and Lisa talk about the kindness of ending Meka's suffering. Gretchen Schoeffler, teary-eyed, tells Melody, "It's the last gift we give them. It's the most unselfish thing we can do." Melody agonizes but then agrees. She asks that all the tubes be removed so she can say good-bye properly.

Free of all the tubes and lines, Meka is free to die. She once again howls—slowly, softly, and mournfully. It is a moment like no other in a room that has witnessed so many dramas.

Lisa injects the pink solution into the neck catheter that will end Meka's life painlessly. Surrounded by the people who love her, Meka dies at 12:30.

After Meka's last breath, George, Melody, and Lisa walk slowly out of the room. Just outside the ICU door, Dr. Lisa Powell, who has fought off the strong emotions that would have hampered her work, can now give in to them.

She and Melody embrace.

It's important later for Lisa to remember shock cases in which, unlike Meka, the animal survived. "One of my favorite cases was an eight-month-old American bulldog. She had just been spayed at a local vet and came in the next day, weak and collapsed. Her gums were very pale," which can indicate blood loss. "Basically, one of the sutures had fallen off inside and she was hemorrhaging."

All the blood that they were transfusing was pouring right back out into her belly. So they did a risky procedure, recommended only in rare cases. "We auto-transfused her." That means they "pulled the blood out of her abdomen and put it right back into her vein." And it looked like it was working. "We just kept doing that and doing that and doing that," Lisa says, "so we could stabilize her for surgery. It was so exciting to see her getting pinker and pinker and pinker."

The risk paid off. "You shouldn't do that [auto-transfuse] too much because there are a lot of complications. For example, if she had an intestinal rupture [the gut is filled with bacteria that should never get loose in the bloodstream], we would have just been getting bacteria back into the blood." It was a last-resort measure, "but in my mind she was just losing it as fast as I could give it to her."

No one would have bet on that dog, but she lived.

* * *

Nishi Dhupa happily remembers another case of septic shock that beat the odds. It was a little rottweiler puppy who was saved not by the big, powerful defibrillating machine, but by a new generation of fluids that can pour life back into dying animals.

The little pup came into the small animal hospital practically a DOA. Nishi recalls, "The owner had called in from home and said the puppy had been vomiting for a few days and that morning just collapsed. So we said, well, rush it in."

But when they got there, the pup was unresponsive. He wasn't breathing. And his little paws had already grown cold.

"Its mucous membranes were white and clammy," Nishi says. "The gums were white, which implies really severe vascular constriction. If you're in a very advanced state of shock, the body shuts down, so you go really white. This little puppy had white or gray membranes and had really cold extremities. If you touched the distal limbs or the ears of a patient like that, they're really freezing cold. And you couldn't feel a pulse on him anywhere. Couldn't hear a heartbeat."

His little body was rising up and down in the jerky movements of agonal breathing—"like a dog that was just about to die," Nishi says. "Because we couldn't feel a pulse and we couldn't actually access a vein, we had to cut down on the jugular. So we cut down very quickly—slashed down. You could see the jugular, and he was cathetered that way."

The most important step was to get life-sustaining fluids in, fast.

"We resuscitated that dog with a couple of those resuscitating fluids. We used something called hypertonic saline. Normal saline is a fluid that we often use that has the same saline concentration as plasma. But hypertonic saline has a concentration that is literally seven times that of plasma. If you inject it as a bolus into the vein of the patient, it's such a high saline concentration that it sucks water in from the tissues. And it acts within fifteen seconds.

This super saline solution gets fluids into the circulatory system the fastest way possible—by robbing them from the tissues. It's a desperate grab at life in a dire situation. The fluids stolen from the tissues can be made up for in the traditional way, via an IV line. Unlike the bloodstream, the body can afford to wait longer for replenishment.

"An intern ran out and told the owners that the pup was basically dead, but that doctors were trying to revive him. The little thing, in fact, was so far gone that we had to do CPR on him and then intubate him, allowing a ventilator to do the work of his failing lungs."

Within ten minutes they had a bizarre tracing on the EKG monitor. They still couldn't hear a heartbeat, but they were picking up electrical activity. That's because a sick heart sometimes has electrical impulses, but it is not strong enough to actually contract. At that point Nishi put the dog on epinephrine. Called a *positive ion trope*, it strengthens the heart muscle and helps it to beat. "We thought, obviously the dog's got a very sick heart muscle, it hasn't had oxygen for a while, but if we could help it out a little bit and get things pumping, then maybe we could bring it back.

"And we did!"

Normally, a dog in this condition would be sedated so that it could remain attached to the ventilator overnight. Nishi explains, "Often, the brain swells during an arrest and subsequent resuscitation efforts. By keeping an animal drugged and on the ventilator, you give the brain time to heal and ease the swelling." But in this case, the owners did not have the money to pay for expensive time on the ventilator.

Without drugs, the little pup woke up and actually began to chew on the breathing tube. His eyes opened a bit and he began blinking. "It probably took us a day or two before we could truly assess him," Nishi says.

He was very weak initially and stumbled about his cage. That was to be expected. But as he gained strength, he continued to bump into things and they realized he was partially blind. Soon, though, the smart little pup learned his limitations and found his way around anyway. In another week, he could see again.

Nishi says it's much harder to bring a dog back once it's gone into the abyss, medically. Considering the success in this case, Nishi reasons that the pup must have just expired the very moment he got to the hospital. "It was one of the few times that we were actually successful, and I think that dog could not truly have been in that state for more than a minute or two.

"I think what saved the day was the ability to give it the saline and the colloids [a special synthetic plasma] very rapidly and to literally 'volume' resuscitate him. He was a success story, and I think he had a treatable underlying disease. He was a healthy puppy prior to it. This was one of the more dramatic ones."

Surprises—Both
Good and Bad

MEDICINE is full of surprises. Emergency medicine, especially so.

Take the case of the beautiful caramel-colored Rhodesian ridgeback who was brought to the hospital with a tender tummy as his only complaint. The first surprise of many in his case was that as soon as he got there, he collapsed stone dead. Dr. Ari Jutkowitz raced over and revived the dog by rhythmically pressing his palms, one on top of the other, on the dog's chest to compress the heart. He also inserted a tube down the animal's throat to deliver life-sustaining oxygen.

Surprise number two: The dog sprang back to life under Ari's quick care. Though the animal was hardly out of the woods, he was diagnosed with GDV.

Air was quickly emptied from the dog's bloated stomach, and after that came surprise number three: the formerly dead dog felt so good, he walked by himself to radiology for X rays to confirm a case of bloat. After surgery, he was home within days, healthy and back to normal.

There are surprises enough for everyone in emergency medicine. Frequently, people misjudge the severity of their pets' problems, misidentifying easily treated conditions as deadly, or calmly carrying in a dying patient, thinking there's a quick fix. Sometimes it's the doctors who are surprised, either by the nature of the illness or by what appears to be the animal's incredible will to live.

Gretchen Schoeffler tells a tale from early in her career of a dog's astounding ability to survive. While working in Georgia, she treated a pit bull who was hit by a car and seriously injured. The dog, a stray who had no ID tags and no collar, was found by strangers who thought the most humane approach would be to put the dog out of his misery. They then shot the ailing dog seven times in the head. It's important to remember the dog was a pit bull. The seven shots of the small-caliber gun merely bounced off the dog's skull. After being brought to the hospital, he hobbled out two days later none the worse for wear. "He just had a horrible concussion and headache and a broken leg," she says. "You just can't kill a pit bull."

Ari agrees. "I treated a little red pit bull once," he says. "It was an awful accident. The dog had been hit by a car and then dragged for a stretch down the road. With half her face scraped off, she looked like Arnold Schwarzenegger in *The Terminator*." Under one eye, her cheekbone was exposed. Much of the dog's skull was laid bare. The fur and skin on her tail were "degloved"—an all-too-descriptive word for what happens when the skin is ripped away from the body, as though pulled off like a glove. What Ari remembers most is that as he treated this poor creature, she never became aggressive. He flushed out the cheek area with fluid, and she just watched him with her soulful eyes and, as he says, "wagged that little bone stub of a tail."

These kinds of wounds look nightmarish, but they can be treated quite successfully. Dr. Nick Dodman recalls the most dramatic degloving incident of his career. "The worst I've ever seen of these was a dachshund," he says. "It was a degloving incident in which the skin just slid right off. It's almost like a skin coming off a sausage, or like pulling a sock off your foot."

The little dog had been run over in her driveway. "The owner had run the car over it and managed to somehow pinch the rear end of the dog under the car tire so that his skin from his chest area just went 'pop.' " Similar to a pair of pants falling around the ankles, the skin bunched around his rear end. "So the whole middle of the dog was just bald like a piece of butcher meat . . . It was hideous.

"It's amazing how they tolerate pain. But with degloving injuries, the skin can be sewn right back on. So we just rinsed everything with saline, pulled the trousers back up, and put a row of stitches right around the whole dog and he healed. It was terrific."

When a dog has been hit by a car, everyone knows it's serious. With other traumas or illnesses, though, signs that seem minor to us are recognized as grave by the veterinary staff. Constipation, for instance, seems like a minor complaint. But in dogs or cats it often signals a major complication—a tumor or blockage.

There are many surprising symptoms that raise a red flag with the critical-care staff. In the ICU circles, the term *down dog* is ominous. When word comes back from a tech or a student that a "down dog" has arrived, it most likely will be an emotionally draining and ultimately tragic situation.

The statistical reality is that if a dog cannot get up on her own, the odds immediately shift against her. And usually the owners are completely unaware how bad the situation is. For a veterinarian in ICU, such a case is a double whammy—a dog you cannot help and an owner who is emotionally unprepared for the devastating report that you must deliver. Over and over in the ICU as a resident takes in a down dog, the eyes of every staff person within hearing range lower.

Dr. Maureen McMichael explains: "Dogs are amazing. If they sprain an ankle, or if they have something wrong with one foot, they run happily on the other three legs, not even knowing that there is anything wrong. They have no clue." She sighs, "But if they're not getting up, it's usually really bad. It's usually something systemic—internal bleeding and they're too weak to get up, or a back fracture or a disc." In that scenario, she says, an injured disc is the best possible problem because out of all the possibilities, it's the most likely to be fixed with surgery.

When Kathleen Conner arrived at the hospital one warm December afternoon, she was concerned but not terribly worried. The weather was pleasantly warm. The thermometer had hit 70 degrees, and made it feel like spring. Kathleen thought she'd take her children and her strikingly fit and handsome black Great Dane Azaria off to York Beach in Maine for a romp. But Azaria had slipped on the kitchen floor and began limping a bit. As any good owner would do, Kathleen kept an eye on her, hoping the problem would work itself out. Soon after, however, Azaria fell again, this time while climbing the back stairs. One of her legs slid through a space between the steps, and she was unable to lift herself out. Kathleen struggled to help the 125-pound dog back up, but Azaria refused to stand after that. Kathleen wondered if it was a sprain or pulled muscle exacerbated by the second fall. Well, so much for the day at the beach, Kathleen thought. She decided not to wait a day to see how things went, but to bring the dog right in for treatment.

It certainly wasn't the first time this Dane had gone to the vet's. In fact, Azaria seemed to be a canine Calamity Jane. The family had spent a fortune on surgery for her in April when she had stomach surgery for GDV. The problem had taken a terrible toll, and Azaria's spleen had to be removed. That meant she had to eat a special soft diet forever afterward.

In addition, Azaria compulsively licked certain areas of her skin, what behaviorists call *lick granuloma*, or canine compulsive disorder. She also had quirky fears, as many of the giant breeds do. The family had to switch all the phones in the house to the cordless kind because Azaria was spooked by the movement of phone cords. She was disturbed by paper bags. And the dog absolutely became unglued around lamb. No one was allowed to cook it in the house because for some unfathomable reason, it drove the dog crazy, making her act fearful. She also hated to get her feet wet and balked at stepping out in snow or rain.

Kathleen was accustomed to helping out this big beautiful dog. So the owner sat in an examining room, wearing sneakers and jeans and a blue sweater, the outfit that was chosen hours before with the intention of enjoying this gift of a warm day by traveling to the ocean. The sleek black dog was stretched out on a blanket, not on a sandy beach but on the cold tiles of the hospital examining room.

A student came in to take the standard preliminary history, asking about the dog's previous medical history and recent behavior. Kathleen was still upbeat. She could only laugh at herself and the lengths she was willing to go to for her beloved dog. Azaria's medical tab this year alone was already running past $2,400—and that wasn't even counting the doorframe she'd pulled off, Kathleen said. Whatever misconceptions she had about Azaria's present ailment, however, were about to be brutally righted.

ICU veterinarian Liz Rozanski enters. She is reserved and serious. She asks Kathleen a series of questions. Have there been any other episodes of slipping like this? No. Any weakness? No. Any subtle neurological changes? No.

In Kathleen's presence, Liz first listens to Azaria's heart and lungs with her stethoscope. Next, she uses a rubber hammer to test Azaria's back legs. When she gets no reflex response, the mood in the room darkens.

Liz tries to get Azaria up, supporting her by the waist. But the back legs of this athletic dog merely hang down limp. Her back paws knuckle under when touched to the floor. The dog is gently placed back down on the blanket.

A test using a small scissor-like clamp called *hemostats* (designed for clamping blood vessels during surgery), pinching tissue up and down the leg and the pads on the bottom of her paws, reveals that Azaria has no sensation in her hind end. She cannot even feel deep pain. Her front legs, too, are becoming rigid.

Before anything is even said to her, Kathleen is realizing that this is not a simple spill.

Liz sighs, unhappy about what she has to say, but she is direct nonetheless. "The signs are about as bad as they can be. And I'm not at all sure it's something we're going to be able to help her with."

It appears that Azaria did not injure herself in a fall; rather, the reverse happened. In humans it used to be believed that elderly women broke their hips by falling, and then it was discovered that often the bone is so weak, it breaks and then the victim falls. So it was here. Something serious was going wrong with Azaria's spinal cord.

Usually, veterinarians can tell where the "insult" to the spine is located by which legs are affected and how they react. Lesions in the spinal column above L3 (lumbar vertebrae 3, just in front of the pelvis) result in weak or paralyzed hind limbs with increased reflexes (knee jerk) and possibly no deep pain. The loss of sensation for deep pain is the last to go in a quickly deteriorating process, and hope is linked to getting medical care before that happens. But that is all too often impossible.

Azaria needs to be anesthetized so that a *myelogram* can be performed. Dye is injected into the spinal column, and it runs down the spine, stopping where there is a blockage, such as a protruding disc. This shows up in the X-ray images taken in series. The problem could be a slipped disc, though not likely. There could be a blood clot or a tumor. Something could be putting pressure on the spine. The worst scenario, and probably the most likely, is bleeding inside the spinal column itself. If the problem is outside the column, there may be ways to fix it. Inside, nothing can be done, and the most humane solution is to put the dog to sleep while she is already under anesthetic.

Kathleen, crying, readily agrees to the test, and she is left alone to spend a few moments with the sensitive dog who seemed so healthy and happy just that morning. Kathleen leaves Azaria to run out to the car for a camera. Despite her red and puffy eyes, she asks a stranger in the hallway to snap a portrait of her with her dog. It will, in fact, be her last.

Later that night, Kathleen will hear of the bad myelogram result by telephone. It is the result everyone feared: bleeding inside the spinal column. She okays euthanasia. Azaria will not come out of her slumber, and Kathleen will be hard pressed even to close her eyes this night. In a mere twelve hours everything turned upside down, and what seemed to be a clumsy misstep signaled the end of a life.

On the flip side, many cases that seem appalling can be cured in the ICU. Take this inspirational case that came in one Christmas day.

Isabelle's injury was one that made people turn away in horror. It was the kind no owner would want to ever contemplate. The delicate and tiny sand-colored one-year-old Chihuahua had been wrestling with another dog at home over a chew toy when her eye got snagged in the tussle and was pulled out of its socket. The medical term is *proptosis* of the eye.

Red, swollen, and protruding way out past her cheek, the eye was gruesome to see. But veterinarians love to brag about these cases. Proptosis is remarkably repairable, and furthermore, many dogs even regain their vision. Added to that, dogs with this condition rarely seem to be in pain. One student tells the story of a Pekingese whose eye was hanging only by a thread of tissue who entered the waiting room wagging his tail, eager to play with other dogs.

Isabelle was not so outgoing. In the ICU, she shook in her little cage as she waited for surgery. The little four-pound pup possessed not only a certain bearing despite the indignity of having her eye hanging out, but she also seemed to exude enough charisma to get people to fuss over her.

Countless staffers stop by her cage to mimic the Taco Bell television ads that sport a fun-loving Chihuahua.

Ari Jutkowitz, known for his sensitivity and compassion, carries little Isabelle back to the non-sterile surgical area known in the vernacular as "dirty surgery." Superficial surgeries that don't require a perfectly sterile environment are done here.

Ari sits cross-legged on the examining table, waiting for the vets who will do the procedure to arrive. As Isabelle shivers in Ari's hands, he holds her close and talks to her.

Within ten minutes, Dr. John MacGregor, an ICU intern, and a fourth-year veterinary student have set up sterile packs of surgical equipment. After a sedative is injected through a vein in her tiny leg, Isabelle goes limp. Laid out on the table, the tiny patient looks even more vulnerable.

An instrument that looks like a metal shoehorn is used to press down her tongue, and a breathing tube to deliver oxygen is put in place. Lying with her bad eye facing up, poor little Isabelle looks like a gargoyle. Ari suggests a heating pad for the small animal lying unconscious in the large, cool room. One is placed beneath her, though heating pads must be monitored closely, since the patient can't complain if it gets too hot.

What the team plans to do next is astonishing. They will medicate the eye with antibiotic cream and then simply suture her eyelids closed over the injured eye. The combination of time, steroids, and antibiotics will reverse the swelling, and the eye will heal back into place. Sometimes when the eye has been pulled even farther out, it is ever so gently nudged back into place.

Since the optic nerve was never severed, when the sutures are removed in two or three weeks, Isabelle may have her full vision back.

In her case, the only hitch is that the eye is so terribly swollen, there isn't quite enough eyelid material to stretch over the eye. Two tiny but painful-looking nicks are made with a blade at the skin just outside the eyeball itself to stretch the eyelid over. Ari says that in four other similar surgeries he's performed, this slit or *canthotomy* was unnecessary, though it is pretty common. A canthotomy, according to the medical texts, can "facilitate globe replacement in some cases."

The suturing is a bit hair-raising because of the danger of hooking the eyeball underneath. During the worst of it, big John MacGregor, delicately wielding the needle, grumbles, "And managers at McDonald's get paid more than I do."

Two small lengths of tiny plastic tubes are placed on the top and bottom eyelids, and the sutures are passed through them. These tubes create a barrier between the taut sutures and the fragile tissue of the lid.

Isabelle comes through surgery fine and goes home the next day. Her three-week recuperation is smooth, too, but unfortunately, sight is not restored in her injured eye.

"That's okay," Ari reports later. Isabelle, he explains, is a beloved lap dog. "She's a little dog whose feet never even touch the ground. She doesn't need to see all that well anyway."

Just as dramatic, and equally tough on the squeamish, are cases of pets suffering from rodenticide poisoning. Rat poison is often tempting to dogs for the same reason it is to rats—to bait the animal, manufacturers make its smell and taste appealing. Warfarin, a common chemical in these poisons, stops an animal's ability to form blood clots and to produce vitamin K. Rats who eat the poison bleed to death. Dogs can die from it, too, unless they get prompt medical attention.

"They look like they're dying, because they are dying," Dr. Maureen McMichael says of the dogs who come in suffering from poisoning.

"Rat poisoning looks really, really bad. I had a dog present with it recently. She was all swollen under the sternum with blood. We didn't know that at the time. She had her arms extended, and they do that when they can't breathe. They sort of open their elbows. She was taking these deep breaths, and blood was just pouring out of her mouth and nose and coming from her lungs. She was bleeding into her lungs."

Though it is a dire situation for the dog, and a desperate sight for a panic-stricken owner, Maureen says, "If you can get them in time, you can give them a plasma transfusion, which has all the coagulation factors that they're missing from the poison. If you can give them that and give them vitamin K, it can reverse everything."

If dogs are bleeding into their lungs, the doctor needs to stop the bleeding immediately. "When they first eat the poison, it doesn't cause any problems at all for up to three to five days. So, the poison seeps throughout their system, and then it starts causing bleeding problems. People don't even connect what the dog did four days ago with what's happening now."

The animals are kept on vitamin K for a long time—a month or six weeks, depending on the kind of poison they've ingested. "The new rat poisons last for over three weeks in the system," Maureen says.

Doctors actually like to get these cases. "It's so good for us once in a while to get one of those," she says, with a laugh at the thought that a poisoning could be called "good." But compared to the ailments they see every day that they cannot fix, poisoning looks like a piece of cake. "I like toxicities," Maureen says, "because they are something you can do something about. In a day where you see fifteen cancers and twelve euthanasias, you need a good toxicity."

Every doctor agrees that a happy ending is always better than a medically intriguing case, but sometimes the two come together. John MacGregor tells of one. A tiny eight-week-old rottweiler pup was brought in close to death. It's excruciating to even contemplate, but the poor baby had had his head shut in a car door. When he arrived at Tufts, he couldn't stand. Far from screaming in pain, the puppy was dull and lethargic, and held his head at a tilt—an ominous sign of neurological damage. But John told the owners he had a chance and quickly put the animal on steroids, medication for pain, and Mannitol, a diuretic to help reduce the swelling of the injured brain. Within three days, the puppy was trotting around and playing. He left the hospital, still with a slight head tilt, but on the mend.

Surprises can be just as astonishing when they take a lot longer. Dr. Terri O'Toole is a medical sleuth. She is a resident in internal medicine, but has spent a great deal of time in the ICU. She intends to become double-boarded, as Dr. Nishi Dhupa already is.

What Terri is already an expert in is patience. She is in a case for the long haul. Rather than feeling frustrated if there is no immediate resolution, she is passionate about keeping an animal going for as long as it takes to figure out and treat the medical mystery (though she is always prepared to recommend euthanasia in clearly hopeless cases). She is bemused that that is not compatible with the temperament of many ICU doctors.

Her long-term efforts with animals are legendary. Fritz the Schnauzer is one of her most famous cases. Terri says,

"They're like little nightmares that nobody wants to put their hands on because they can go bad at any time. You just walk through them with the owners, keeping your fingers crossed."

Little Fritz was about six when he first came to Tufts. He had been referred to the hospital by his local vet, who had diagnosed Fritz with a fairly common disorder called IMHA, or *immune mediated hemolytic anemia*. In this situation the immune system goes haywire and destroys red blood cells, vital units that carry oxygen in the blood. Fritz had also been treated for colitis because he had bloody stools. And on top of all that, because of a high dose of antibiotics he had gotten previously, he was suffering from what is called *bone marrow failure*—in which his bone marrow shut down and simply stopped producing red blood cells altogether.

Terri says, "He wasn't making any red cells, wasn't making white cells, wasn't making platelets. We thought he had bone marrow failure because the medication he was getting was causing a toxic insult. It was a very high dose, and he'd been on it before." This was important because it is during a second round of therapy that IMHA can set in. "We hoped that if we took him off the Tribissen, his bone marrow would come back."

Because the doctor had diagnosed IMHA, he had also put Fritz on prednisone, a synthetic steroid that suppresses the immune system. Prednisone, given in high doses, must be tapered off gradually—it cannot be simply shut off at once. Though Terri wanted to get Fritz off the prednisone, she had to do it slowly.

Fritz started to feel better from treatment. His bone marrow came back, and a month later, he returned to Tufts for a recheck. What Terri saw this time, through lab work, seemed to confirm that indeed Fritz had IMHA. The clinical evidence pointed in that direction, too. As the prednisone was reduced and the immune system was not as suppressed, he was once again losing red blood cells.

"He had these spherocytes [cells that indicate immune damage to red cells], and he was autoagglutinating," in which red cells clump together due to antigen-antibody interactions. That indicates dysfunction in the immune system.

Simultaneously, the low platelet count was making Terri wonder about liver problems. Lab results showed very high liver enzyme values, and she wondered if the drugs Fritz had been on previously were causing toxicity in that organ.

"So we started him on a separate drug called Imuran, hoping we could get him down off the prednisone to see if his liver was prednisone-related as well," Terri says.

Because he had been on such high doses of so many medications, which in and of themselves can cause problems, she couldn't tell what was disease and what was reaction to medications.

As Terri waited for the prednisone levels to drop, Fritz had a sudden episode in which he began to vomit violently. He appeared quite ill to his owner. Terri's concern now was that the Immuran, which was given to him to suppress his immune system, was now causing pancreatitis, or inflammation of the pancreas. Unfortunately, it coincided precisely with a period of time in which Terri was studying for her boards and she was out of the hospital entirely.

Terri had another vet in her section see Fritz, but by that time Fritz was spontaneously better. Nonetheless, as a precaution, the vet ordered an ultrasound of the dog's belly. Normally, the pancreas cannot be seen well in an ultrasound, but when it is inflamed, it's painfully visible. Fritz's entire abdominal area looked perfectly normal on the screen, and the dog went home.

Yet the doctor also had Fritz donate a urine sample for analysis. That was fortunate, because it signaled yet another problem. "He was spilling a lot of protein in his urine," Terri says. That indicated kidney dysfunction. Because she was considering a liver biopsy on the dog anyway, her colleague suggested she also do one on the kidney.

At the same time, the prednisone dose was raised again, because the medical team believed that the IMHA was destroying his platelets—small disc-shaped bodies that are an important part of blood clot formation—along with his red blood cells. But despite the increase of steroids, his platelet count never increased.

A biopsy just might hold the key to the puzzles, but the owner got cold feet. What if the surgery ended up actually making him feel worse? she wondered anxiously. After all, her poor dog had already been through so much. "Owners will often say if there's a chance it will make them worse, I don't want to do it. That makes your decision pretty easy," Terri says.

Now it was time for her to play a familiar role—Sherlock Holmes, DVM. Like any detective, Terri had to use the evidence available to make up a plausible story medically for the biological crime taking place. She mulled over all the evidence, and formed her theory.

Maybe Fritz "threw a clot," that is, a blood clot formed someplace internally that blocked digestion. That made the dog sick and vomit. Because platelets had been exhausted in forming this clot to begin with, there were few left circulating in his system. That would explain the low platelet count. The high protein count in the urine would make sense considering the underlying problem of immune problems affecting the kidney. Then, when the blood clot dissolved and digestion returned to normal, before Fritz could even get to the vet, he would naturally feel better.

A tight, logical theory. But was it true?

One way to confirm some of this without a risky biopsy would be to check the antithrombin level. Antithrombin is a natural anti-clotting agent in the body. It is a small molecule, and when the kidney is losing proteins, antithrombin is lost as a part of that process. If levels are low, the patient is more likely to "throw" clots to various organs, such as the kidney, lung, and spleen. This sophisticated test would have to be sent out to Cornell, and it would take about a week for the results to come back.

A short time later, on a day off, no less, Terri came into the hospital to sit in on the big weekly ICU staff meeting. There in her mailbox, she found the lab results for Fritz.

She remembers the report vividly. "Thursday night, the antithrombin level is back in my box, and it's desperately low," Terri says. "Normal is 70 to 120 percent and Fritz is 26 percent. Desperately low. And I'm wondering what I should do about this. I went home, because rounds finished up around eight. On Friday, my second day off, the owner beeps me and says Fritz is not quite right today. He's been vomiting, he doesn't want to eat, and he's lethargic. He won't play with his toys." The clincher was when the owner said that last night Fritz was breathing like he had run a marathon. Terri was convinced that the dog had thrown a clot to his lung. That was very bad news. People die from those. Dogs do, too.

Terri is growing more and more concerned. "I said, I think you need to bring him up. I'm going to call ahead and tell the doctor that's on tonight, who was Maureen, and I'll be there tomorrow."

Terri felt compelled to warn the owner how serious this problem could be. When blood clots get loose in the bloodstream, they can plug up circulation anywhere, often in the most dangerous places. "I have to admit I got a little teary-eyed when I hung up the phone, because this was one of my deeply involved cases. And all of a sudden I thought it might go bad."

Terri came in early the next morning and found Fritz in an oxygen chamber—"the O_2 cage." He looked fairly healthy and a chest X ray taken during the night looked perfectly normal. That did not fit with the suspicion of a clot in his lungs, but it was still possible. Terri prescribed Coumadin and Heparin to stop clot formation and break up any existing clots.

"He was pretty comfortable Saturday," Terri says, but "Sunday his belly started to get distended, and he was breathing hard. It was different from before—there was a grunt with every breath, like his belly hurt."

Fritz's owner was there that Sunday afternoon and she began to cry, seeing her dog in such discomfort. Making things worse was the knowledge that there was no definitive diagnosis, and therefore no surefire treatment. She began to wonder if she should put Fritz out of his misery.

As Terri was talking with her client, she had an idea. "I wonder if he's thrown a clot to his gut, and he's infarcting his bowel, which is terrible." An infarction, the death of tissue in a particular area, occurs when the blood supply is shut off to it. The tissue dies from lack of oxygen being delivered by the blood.

"I said, why don't I take him down and X-ray him." But, again, the films just led to more questions. "His X rays showed that he had loops of bowel that were full of fluid," Terri explains. But if it had been an infarction, those loops would be full of air, not fluid.

She returned to her earlier idea, that a pulmonary thrombo embolism clot was blocking his lung. It was not unreasonable to suspect that the problem in his abdomen was related.

A radiology resident happened by just then, and Terri corralled her. The resident was skeptical of Terri's theory and told her so. Still, the radiology resident reluctantly agreed to shave Fritz's belly and take a look at his insides with the ultrasound equipment.

Within minutes, the resident was running through the hallways looking for Terri. "There are clots everywhere!" she told Terri. "He's infarcted his kidney, he's infarcted his mesenteric artery, he's infarcted his spleen, there's a clot here, there's a clot there, he's got clots everywhere!"

That meant, for some reason, Fritz was forming clots throughout his system. They were causing infarctions in several organs. It was a wonder Fritz wasn't dead already.

Terri had to approach the distraught owner and tell her the frightening news. Her dog was having what's called a *thrombotic accident*.

"I said, this is really bad, and I don't know how to treat this massive thrombotic accident. We never see it. Usually when it happens, dogs just die mysteriously and we don't know why."

Now they could see it happening before their very eyes. But how to stop it was the big question. The only thing to do was to launch an all-out attack, hoping to dissolve all the clots overnight somehow.

The most worrisome clot was located in the liver, one of the largest organs, and a terribly important one. It provides a number of services for the system: it detoxifies blood; is central to the storage of sugars, iron, and vitamins; aids in digestion; helps produce proteins and antibodies; and aids in waste management.

"Fritz had this huge clot in the blood vessels draining the lungs, and when this happens in people, it's usually death. Instant death," Terri says.

The fluid in Fritz's abdomen now made sense medically. His gut was dying, and nothing was moving around in his digestive tract as it should have been.

"I put him on a bunch of antibiotics, knowing that his gut was dying," Terri says. The digestive tract has lots of good, natural bacteria that helps with digestion. But if it spills into the bloodstream it can be deadly.

"I started him on thrombolytic therapy to break up the clots and oxyglobin, to help deliver oxygen to the hypoxic tissue." Oxyglobin is a new blood substitute, recently licensed for use in dogs and it may be available for humans soon. She put him back in the oxygen chamber.

All that was happening is unheard of in the literature. There was nothing to guide the vet.

"I'm just making this up as I go along," Terri says. "What can I do? The owner was game to give him one more night, and I gave him pain medication and left him in the oxygen cage."

That one night extended to several.

Dr. Nishi Dhupa, who had been away on vacation, returned to work, and she and Terri put their heads together, trying to devise the best strategy to dissolve the clot in the liver.

"We talked to surgeons, we talked about doing ultrasound vibrations to break up the clots," Terri says. However, the very expensive ultrasound therapy equipment could only be found in human hospitals, and it seemed unlikely the surgeons would go along with it.

But before any of that became necessary, a combination of Coumadin and antibiotics began to do the trick. Slowly the dog got better. After a few days, Fritz got to go home.

He made it. But that wasn't the end of the story. On recheck a week later, it appeared that everything was going smoothly, and, most important, the clot in the liver area had shrunk significantly. The owner reported that Fritz was nearly himself again—90 percent well was her estimate.

But a few weeks later, around the Fourth of July, the owner reported something a little strange. "She says, Fritz is doing great but he won't sleep through the night. He's up in the night—anxious," Terri recalls.

Terri told her she was stumped, but as long as Fritz was otherwise fine, it didn't seem like much to worry about.

"I don't know why this went through my head," Terri says, "but I started thinking about alcoholics when they get end-stage liver failure." Their livers have shrunk and are no longer functioning properly. Long unused blood vessels between the liver and the abdominal blood supply tend to reopen. The main roads in and out of these emaciated livers don't function well, and all these other little abnormal vessels open up.

Why is this sinister? "They open up these teeny little shunts everywhere," Terri explains. The consequences are devastating. Ammonia, which is a byproduct of proteins being broken down in the digestive system, no longer get detoxified as they should in the liver. "The liver is supposed to get rid of ammonia." But in this case the liver doesn't get the ammonia to detoxify it because it's circumventing the organ and going out through the shunts. "So when ammonia escapes the liver and it's in the regular circulation, it goes to the brain, where it acts as a toxin to the nervous system. Alcoholics with end-stage liver failure become what we call 'encephalopathic' because ammonia is in their brain acting as a neurotoxin."

Terri shared her notion with Fritz's owner. "It could be that he threw a clot to his heart, and he's got an arrhythmia [irregular heartbeat]. Maybe he's hypertensive because of his kidney disease. His blood pressure is high, and he's just acting weird because of that." Then she mentioned her latest idea, that Fritz might be suffering from high ammonia levels "because that's what they say with alcoholics. They can't sleep at night. You treat them for their ammonia, and then they can sleep."

The next step was to test Fritz for ammonia levels in his system. When he came in, Terri took blood, did an EKG to test his heart, and took his blood pressure.

The EKG was fine, the blood pressure was normal, and lo and behold, his ammonia was high. The drunken dog theory was accurate.

Fritz was put on a low-protein diet to prevent more ammonia buildup. But he didn't mind the restriction—he was getting a lot of toast and ice cream.

His owner soon reported that her dog was happy and normal and 100 percent Fritz.

Terri says the clot in his liver has shrunk dramatically. The pleural vein has returned to its normal size. On a third ultrasound, they finally discovered the liver shunt that was causing all the problems. Even that has shriveled up and stopped misbehaving. Fritz is on regular dog food and off all medicines.

"Now the shunt is gone, his antithrombin level is normal, and he is no longer losing protein in his urine," Terri happily reports.

So what started the whole problem? And what is the name of the disease?

"I don't know what was wrong with him," she says. "It could have been a strange allergy. An immune reaction. Lupus which is now in remission. No one can know." Colleagues have enthusiastically encouraged Terri to write up Fritz's story in the medical literature, but Terri laughs. "I still don't know what he has."

Naming his medical problem was and is less important to Terri than saving Fritz. The same is true for the dog's owner.

"Any owner by any normal reasoning could have put this dog to sleep at any time, but she just kept sticking with him," Terri says.

There are surprises in the ICU that shock not only the owner and vet, but sometimes the entire medical establishment. Nick Dodman recalls one of those cases—a medical novelty with a twist. "I was on general surgery, at an emergency clinic in Glasgow," he says, "when a woman and man came in with a little dog. The dog was clearly lame in the back leg." The woman was carrying something on a little square of "grease-proof" paper—the kind you get a sandwich or takeout chicken in.

"The woman says, 'The reason I'm here is my dog was struck by a car and its bone flew out and here it is.'" She unwrapped the piece of paper with a flourish, and there in the center was a little bone that looked suspiciously like a drumstick.

"I was beginning to smile a little bit to myself," Nick reports. "I said, where did you find it?" She drew him a map of the accident scene and said, "Twenty yards back down the yard in the gutter we found the bone. We're wondering if perhaps there is some way of reinserting it or something."

Nick stifled a laugh, and gravely picked up the bone and the dog, saying he would see what he could do.

"I walked the dog down to X ray and had the X ray people take the film," Nick says. They were all giggling over the notion that this little drumstick had popped clean out of the dog's leg.

But then the techs said, "Hey, doc! Come over here and look at it." Nick lifted the film to the light panel and, sure enough—no bone.

"It was completely gone," Nick marvels, "all the way from its hip down to its knee. The whole shaft of his femur was not there." The ends of this long bone were still in place. It was the center length, the shaft, that was missing.

What had happened, he deduced, was that the dog had been hit by the car on the knee and that the shaft had been pushed out through a tiny hole. It shot straight out through this hole vertically up, flipped around in the air and the owner saw it exiting. The hole was only as wide as the bone, about a half inch. Its fur had then covered over the tiny exit wound.

"I disbelieved her, and I shouldn't have. We took her to the orthopedic surgeons and I said, 'What are you going to do about this?' They're all very good with their pins and wires and bits and screws and things like this—but there was nothing to pin or wire.

They decided they couldn't send her home without the leg bone, so they put the dog in a small cat cage where it wouldn't be able to exercise or jump up and down and traumatize the injury. "They said we'll just keep it and see what happens."

They X-rayed it serially, once a week, and soon they were amazed to see, the X rays showed "this thin white line joining the top of her epiphysis [cap of bone at the joint] with the bottom. What it must have been was the membrane that surrounds the bone, the periosteum, which is responsible for some bone growth, produced calcification."

Within weeks the dog was walking and could be sent home. Monitoring through many checkups, the vets witnessed—remarkably—that the thin white line of calcification grew stronger and thicker with time.

The case was written up in *The Journal of Small Animal Practice* in 1979. Titled "An unusual example of fracture healing," the abstract reads, "The authors report the natural healing of a fractured femur in a young puppy where the whole diaphysis had been lost." The publication included incredible photos of the natural bone bridge. It concluded, "Although this is probably a unique case and unlikely to occur again, it is a useful illustration of the potential healing ability of the small animal patient."

"It was pretty rough. I mean, it looked very gnarly, like the root on a tree, " Nick says. "But there it was, and the dog was completely sound."

TOUGH DECISIONS: WHEN TO END THE SUFFERING AND WHEN TO KEEP TRYING

SOME animals, no matter how sick they are, seem to charm everyone in the ICU. Glover, the gray tiger cat, was that kind of patient. Double-pawed and mellow, the petite eleven-year-old cat was made for snuggling.

She also, unfortunately, was the kind of case ICU staffers see more of than they can sometimes bear. Glover had a problem they couldn't cure.

Intensive care units at any veterinary hospital have very high mortality rates. The animals coming to the ICU have sustained the worst kinds of trauma, the most virulent kinds of infections, and the most mysterious ailments that other vets cannot diagnose. Some patients are actually already dead when they get there.

It's not unheard of for an admitting resident to see every patient die within a shift. It's part of the job. Certain animals they know right away cannot be saved. Others, like Glover, are medical mysteries, whose illnesses may reveal themselves through progressive tests. That also means, however, the doctors spend more time with the animal, bond more, and get their own hopes up.

The day Glover came in had been a tough and busy one in the ICU, and it was fitting when one of the residents complained that the hospital had run out of the small, inexpensive cardboard coffins in which grieving owners carry home dead pets for burial.

Gretchen could be seen talking through the bars of an ICU cage to a marmalade-colored cat with enormous green eyes. A large tumor protruded from the cat's jaw. "I won't feel too bad about putting you to sleep," she cooed. "You've had a good old life."

A big Bernese Mountain dog lay on a bed on the floor. Scheduled to go to surgery for intestinal bleeding, the dog had developed respiratory problems that had to be adressed first.

It wasn't even noon yet.

Into this scene, Maureen McMichael starts her shift. In white lab coat, blue scrubs, and with her glasses and blond ponytail, Maureen has the enviable ability to appear simultaneously hip and studious.

She sees in blue magic marker on the status board in the hallway that a cat named Glover is in and the complaint is vomiting blood. She gets a quick overview from a student, peruses Glover's file, and heads into the examining room where Glover's owner waits.

Glover, a gray cat with white "gloves," is in the ICU receiving a blood transfusion. A, B, and AB are the blood types for cats, with A being the most common here in the United States (it's B in the U.K.).

Karen Azevedo and her sister Kim are perched on the room's small wooden bench. The two redheads are well dressed, and they look alike—twin nineties versions of Debbie Reynolds; they even have her kind of pizzazz. Maureen introduces herself and asks a few questions about Glover. Karen says that Glover has been vomiting once a week for two months. Initially, her kidney values were slightly elevated.

Among the recent changes the cat experienced were a shift in diet and getting a loose tooth pulled. Neither helped. Her vomiting actually increased, now occurring every day. The vet suggested changing Glover's feeding schedule, but that didn't help, either. Karen brought her to a cat specialist who "pulled a panel" (a series of blood tests). Her BUN (blood urea nitrogen) level was normal and the creatinine almost normal. These lab tests are used to evaluate kidney function. The vet had also taken X rays and a partial barium series. Nothing was conclusive, and a week ago, Glover simply stopped eating.

Maureen views the X rays, but tells Karen that the barium had not sufficiently defined the problem. Checking the white-blood cell count and hematocrit shows how anemic Glover is.

Maureen examines Glover back in ICU and reports to Karen that she can feel a mass in Glover's abdominal area. "Sometimes it's just feces in the colon," Maureen says, "and you can gently squish it, but I couldn't define it." Preliminary blood work here reveals that Glover is anemic, and her gum color is poor—a very pale pink. As mentioned earlier, checking the gums is one of the first things doctors do. It is a good indicator of general health. Nice pink gums that blanch white and then regain color quickly after being pressed indicate good blood flow and fast, healthy capillary "refill time." Pale gums point toward anemia (decrease of red blood cells) or the constriction of blood vessels, as appears with shock. Yellow gums tell the vet that the patient may be experiencing liver problems; the yellow pigment bilirubin accumulates in the blood instead of being excreted in feces and urine.

The next step, Maureen explains, is an abdominal ultrasound. That will provide, hopefully, a clear picture of what's happening inside Glover, and it will show whether she is a good candidate for surgery.

Maureen heads back to the ICU to pick up Glover. Dr.

Nishi Dhupa is holding the cat and gently examining her abdomen. Glover seems relaxed in her arms. Continuing her exam, Nishi presses down firmly on the cat's belly. "It could be gastric," Nishi says. "It is *huge.*"

Maureen tells Nishi they are headed for ultrasound and that the only abnormal sign in the blood work so far is a reduced red-blood cell count.

Glover is carried to the darkened ultrasound room, where two technicians, Amy and Sam, are waiting. Glover is placed on her back in the trough of a blue V-shaped, vinyl-coated pad on the table. She has her belly shaved and a cold blue gel squirted on the bare skin. She lies quietly, her tail twitching back and forth. "She's either a very good or a very sick kitty," one of the techs says while stroking the stoic cat.

As the instrument is placed on her glistening belly, a black-and-white picture appears on the monitor. It looks like an undersea search for the Loch Ness Monster. Sam is holding Glover's legs up and petting her chest. Amy talks through what she sees.

The first kidney to surface on the screen looks small. Is it chronic renal disease? As she moves the wand, the other kidney appears. This one is normal. They move toward the mass and find it. The large round shape is in the stomach. But the critical question is, is the mass separate and removable, or is it part of the stomach and unremovable?

All of them know what they want to see: a distinct tumor that can be snipped out. But in the gray, murky world of ultrasound, it is hard to distinguish the masses on the screen.

Sounding defeated, Amy says, "Okay, the mass is part of the stomach. . . . Oh, man, I think it all becomes one." She moves the instrument around, trying views from many directions. The colon is empty, which makes it harder to read. There is some hope that the mass is in the colon. The colon can be resected, meaning that Maureen can chop out a segment containing a tumor and stitch the healthy tissue on either side back together. As dire as that sounds, it is the most hopeful diagnosis that could be made at this point.

Glover is growing uncomfortable, but soft words and a little stroking get her to settle right down. After a few more angles on the screen, everyone is in agreement. They are seeing exactly what they had hoped they wouldn't: the mass is definitely part of the stomach wall. It cannot be removed from the organ, and Glover cannot live without a stomach.

Maureen picks up her patient and gently strokes her soft fur. Glover, so calm and loving, has no idea what the doctor has just learned. Out in the hallway, Maureen finds Dr. Terri O'Toole. Maureen, cradling Glover, goes over her history with Terri, hoping against hope that there is some procedure she hasn't thought of.

Unquestionably, it is cancer, but is it definitely lymphoma? They could aspirate the mass itself, or a nearby lymph node. Lymphoma is a systemic disease, and a common cat cancer that requires surgery to remove the tumor and chemotherapy to stop the spread. Considering that Glover is not eating and she is vomiting blood, these drugs would be very tough on her.

"The best you could hope for with GI lymphoma," Terri says quietly, "is remission. And that would be six months, maybe a year."

Maureen sighs. It, of course, is what she'd thought already.

"If it were my cat, what would I do?" Terri says. "If my kitty cat had GI lymphoma, unless he was eating, I'm not sure. It can be such a struggle." Terri mentions another patient, Kathleen, a fifteen-year-old orange cat with a pelvic mass. With only prednisone as a treatment, Kathleen enjoyed "pretty good quality time for five months," Terri says.

Maureen brings Glover back to a cage in the ICU so the cat can relax. Then she heads back to the room where Karen and her sister are waiting. Maureen explains what the ultrasound has revealed. She tells Karen the most likely scenario is that Glover is suffering from lymphoma. A number of tests, including a biopsy and a bone marrow aspirate, can be done to verify this. The aspirate, taken from bone marrow usually in the femur, would determine the stage of the disease. If detected in bone marrow, it has spread and involves leukemia, too, making the prognosis worse.

The tests are invasive and expensive, starting at $1,000. Even with an otherwise healthy cat, the outlook is limited—probably six months.

There are less invasive, less expensive courses that can be taken, such as treating with prednisone. However, that in itself can cause internal bleeding. Glover is very ill, and the mass is probably causing painful ulcers.

Karen looks at her sister Kim. "What I won't do is keep Glover alive just for my sake," Karen says as she begins to cry. Kim reaches out to her and gets teary, too. "If I take her home and try the medication, is that fair to her?" Karen asks. Clearly, she is asking herself this question as much as Maureen. These are the questions only an owner can answer. How much is my pet suffering? What is her quality of life?

Maureen will not tell Karen what to do, but she will help her to find the right solutions for herself and Glover. "Think of the worst-case scenario with either choice," Maureen says. "If you put her to sleep now, will you question whether you should have given her a chance? And if you try a treatment, invasive or not, and she doesn't do well . . ." Maureen's voice trails off.

"To see her the way she is now," Karen says, shaking her head. "She just goes off to lie on her little hammock. I've been seeing blood, and I'm afraid to see more."

"It's a lot to take in," Maureen says as she puts a box of tissues between the two sisters. "Why don't I leave you guys alone to talk about it for a few minutes?"

As technology catches up with our desire to prolong the life of our pets, increasingly we have to face up to some hard choices. With chemotherapy, amputations, radiation, dialysis, and transfusions, we can keep animals alive. Americans are spending $11 billion each year on the medical care of our pets. But we always have to ask how much we diminish the quality of life when we do this.

We have to size up the very dogness or catness of our pets and no matter how many experts advise us, we alone must make these overwhelming life-or-death decisions for these little creatures we love beyond measure. What all the experts say is that no matter what we decide, there will be some guilt. Financial concerns can compound the recriminations.

These decisions are emotional, for the staff as well as the owners. It reaches deep inside a person and draws out all kinds of feelings about illness and loss and love. Our decisions are often colored by personal experiences with sickness and loss in our own families.

In two cases of dogs with osteosarcoma, a fast-moving, painful cancer of the bone, very different decisions were made because of the unique histories of the owners. The man who had just watched his mother die from colon cancer could not bear to put his Great Pyrenees through chemotherapy. Meanwhile, a woman who had beat the odds herself after almost dying from lupus wants everything possible done to give her Irish wolfhound a chance.

Out in the hallway, Maureen waits and talks about her own dog and how tough the decision would be with him. But she knows, as all pet owners do, that the day will come. With each of her clients, she says, she tries to understand them and their relationship with their pet. She attempts to get a sense of how they feel. "The hardest thing is, I think, not saying anything until you get a clue as to where they're leaning," she says. "I never want to prematurely push anyone in any direction. But when I hear their leanings, I can encourage them toward that. Everybody is different. Some people absolutely have to do everything possible. I recently had a client like this, and her dog had a really bad prognosis, but she really needed to do everything. And I picked up on this."

Maureen did what the owner wanted. "She went through surgery, she went through everything she could, and she took her dog home. He died three days later, which we kind of knew was going to happen, but she was still happy that she, in her mind, had done everything she could have possibly done for him."

After five minutes, Maureen comes in to talk to Karen and Kim again. The two sisters not only look alike, they are very close emotionally. Kim feels that she waited too long with a cat of her own and the two women think that Glover has had a good life, but at this point has suffered enough. For them, prolonging her life seems selfish.

Karen is not afraid. Sad, yes. Our relationships with our pets are often the most perfect of our lives: free of conflict, free of issues. They love us whether we can remember the punch line to a joke or not. We're everything to them, job promotion or not. And they look as lovingly at us when we first wake up in the morning as when we are dressed for a dinner party. It's tough to say good-bye.

Maureen describes the euthanasia process and tells Karen it will be painless for Glover. She asks if Karen would like to be present, and Karen tearfully says yes, she would like to hold her sweet cat in her arms while it's being done.

While Maureen excuses herself to prepare the solution of sodium phenobarbital, Karen talks about Glover.

The little cat had arrived on her doorstep two days after Thanksgiving, no more than a ball of fluff. Her husband didn't want a cat and had objected to keeping her, but he gave in. Glover's white double paws, which looked so much like boxing gloves, got to him. "Everyone loves Glover," she says. Even though Karen is an interior decorator, she indulged Glover's fondness for her ratty, disreputable kitty hammock.

Despite newer ones with thicker padding, Glover loves her old piece of feline furniture.

The two sisters even share a laugh about two elderly women they passed in the waiting room earlier in the day. "There we are in thirty years!" Karen and Kim say. They are laughing and crying, preparing themselves emotionally for what is about to happen. Kim already knows how hard it can be—she fainted the first time she ever had a cat put to sleep.

Maureen enters with Glover in her arms. She hands her over to her owner. She curls into Karen's lap and Karen's eyes fill up with tears. Glover's tail is thrashing as it had in ultrasound, and Karen says she always does that. She looks deep into the clear green eyes of her cat and says, "You're going to wag your tail till the very end, aren't you?"

Maureen asks if they're ready and then pulls out a syringe filled with the most innocuous-looking pink fluid. She finds a vein in Glover's forearm and depresses the plunger. Karen is cradling Glover as the cat's breathing stops.

Karen sobs, stroking the still animal's lush fur. "She always had such a healthy coat," Karen says. Through tears, Kim takes Karen's arm and laughs a bit, "She still does."

As Karen sits with Glover's warm body resting in her lap, Maureen says that she once had a Native American client who told her that the soul stays with the body for five minutes. "I always wait now," Maureen says, to make sure the soul gets a peaceful send-off.

The two sisters cry together, their arms touching. There are several moments of tearful silence. Maureen, moved by the scene, says to Karen, "I hope I can be as unselfish when the time comes."

Maureen and all the vets in the ICU have seen more death than they would have cared to. Some days you can steel yourself; others make it more difficult to fend off overwhelming feelings of sadness.

"Our situation here in the ICU," Nishi says, "is front-line emotion. Eventually, everyone does learn to detach to some degree. But I often end up carrying the thoughts away with me. At home, at night, almost invariably I'll remember it and have a sad moment."

Earlier in her career, Nishi struggled with these emotions, as do all young vets. "I can remember howling over cases in my residency," she says, smiling at the thought of herself just six years ago.

"There was a bull terrier that stands out in my mind," Nishi says. "It was a white, funny-looking dog. To this day, if I see a white bull terrier in the hospital, I choke up instantly. I could cry all over again—it's amazing."

The dog had been quite ill, vomiting for days, when the owners brought him in. He was operated on to remove a foreign body from his intestine, some object he had swallowed that got stuck. A massive infection had already set in. The intestinal tissue had broken down, and the suture sites kept coming apart. Over the course of a week "we went back to surgery four times," Nishi says. The brave little dog didn't make it.

Despite her own emotions, Nishi believes it's her duty to comfort the owners as much as possible. "I think when we are advising clients to put animals to sleep, in those thirty minutes we spend with them, we can make a huge difference to the rest of their lives."

Maureen remembers one day when every case that came through was a dying pet requiring euthanasia. She was wrung out and exhausted emotionally by early afternoon. Then a young woman in her twenties arrived with an old German shepherd. She had had the dog through her teenage years and into adulthood.

"It's sad," Maureen says, recalling the day. "The dog was brought in because of an abdominal mass. On ultrasound, we noticed that the mass looked like a splenic tumor, and it was bleeding into his belly. In German shepherds it's real common."

The spleen is an organ that can be removed successfully, but the type of problem the German shepherd was experiencing, Maureen explains, "is really a tumor of the blood vessels of the spleen, and by the time you've seen it in an ultrasound, and when they've bled into the abdomen, all the little tumor cells are everywhere, so they don't usually have a good prognosis after surgery. Their life span is something like two months. With chemo, they can probably extend it to four to six maybe. So it's a bad cancer." Maureen took the big dog off to radiology. "We took chest X rays and it was all over his lungs, so that's ever worse."

The young woman had first gone to her regular vet when the dog collapsed. Maureen says the tumors, which resemble blood-filled grapes on the spleen, sometimes rupture and bleed, and it can take so long to clot that the dog collapses from blood loss. Maureen had the impression that the owner was not aware of how serious the situation was. Perhaps the local vet, in the process of softening the blow, had not conveyed the urgency of the situation. Sometimes, too, Maureen reports, clients discount what their regular vets have said, and hope the experts at Tufts will have a better prognosis for them.

After a morning of pain and sorrow for so many, Maureen faced a nice owner again who had no idea how grave her dear dog's condition was. What could she do?

"So, I told her," Maureen says with a sigh. "She didn't have the money to do the surgery, and it was a pretty poor prognosis anyway." Maureen looks defeated even remembering this scene.

"It was a bad day, it was an exhausting day, a lot of euthanasias. So, I told her all of these things about the dog's condition, and she just sat there stoically listening, nodding her head. Then she said she would take him home for the little time he had left and take him to her regular vet when the time came." Maureen reveals, "I felt so guilty. I was relieved that it wasn't turning into a big emotional thing. I didn't have any energy left at all, which is really sad."

Of course, it is precisely because Maureen is such a compassionate vet that she felt as drained as she did. It was precisely why she was angry with herself for not prodding this woman more to make sure she really was all right with the terrible news she had just heard.

Maureen set up all the paperwork, and the young woman left. Maureen began her next case, a cat owned by an elderly couple, "the cutest couple in the world," she recalls. But karma was just catching up. "I guess there's no free lunch," Maureen says, "so I couldn't get away with it."

Only the husband came in to see Maureen. He said his wife was wandering around. Since she was prone to do this, the husband and wife always carried cell phones with them. That way the husband could always contact his wife. "She's not answering, though," he told Maureen with a little consternation. "She was just walking in the parking lot."

After her upsetting morning, Maureen felt that she could use a breath of fresh air. I'll go out and look for your wife, she told the husband. How many elderly women with cell phones ringing in their pockets could there be? she thought.

"I did find her," Maureen says. "She was by a car talking to the young woman I had just sent out with the German shepherd. They were both crying, and the older woman was comforting the girl. And it was so sad, just so sad. She was there just crying and crying. Well, the three of us ended up talking and crying."

Once more, Maureen opened herself up to sharing in the pain of a person losing a best friend. In fact, the cat that the elderly people brought in was suffering from a brain tumor and had to be put to sleep that day. In this case though, Maureen says the older couple comforted one another and handled it "beautifully."

No one could question Karen's decision to let Glover die with dignity that day. But there are plenty of cases that prompt questioning. Animals who have simple problems are put to sleep because of financial considerations. Some are put down because the owners can't face the amount of care the pet will require. Sometimes, people question those who go to the limit to save a pet. In this day of such advanced technology at sophisticated hospitals like Tufts, we often may ask, how much is too much?

Terri O'Toole is "dogged" in her determination to care for animals who come to her. Yet she is also forthright in suggesting euthanasia in cases for which there is no hope. One of the least outwardly emotional vets on staff, Terri nonetheless has come into conflict with colleagues on more than one occasion over her determination to treat animals that others feel should be put down.

In one of these cases, Terri kept a three-legged, blind, neurologically damaged cat alive, not only giving her medical care in the hospital, but also taking the cat home to nurse it back to health in her private time. A committee set up in the hospital to monitor such issues disagreed with her decision. But Terri eloquently makes her case.

Squeakers was a four-year-old, three-legged cat who came into the ICU the night before Thanksgiving. She was wracked by a series of unrelenting seizures. "They were just one on top of another," Terri recalls.

Cats experience many types of seizures. "They can look like the regular seizure that you recognize, in which they fall over on their side. They're not conscious or responsive. But cats can also have seizures where they just sit and they're very still and their whiskers twitch or their ears twitch. The eyes might be watering a little bit," Terri says. "They shake or get very tense. They can urinate, defecate, and/or vomit."

Squeakers' behavior was out of control—violent movements including frantic leaps into the air.

"Actually, for people that's not uncommon," Terri says, "when they come from the temporal lobe or the frontal lobe. They call them temporal lobe epilepsy or frontal lobe epilepsy, where they violently jump up, they can twist and spin. Sometimes they call them psychomotor, where they are hallucinating, like seeing flying saucers. Something will fly over their head, or they'll think something is on their back."

That's how it was for Squeakers. "She was having these violent leaping-in-the-air, vocalizing seizures," Terri relates. "She had been to a local vet for bad seizures the last couple of days, and the vet had given her typical kinds of anticonvulsant drugs." Squeakers did not respond to them, and the doctor that admitted her could not control the seizures either and put her on Propafol, a sedating drug used to anesthetize outpatients.

The problem with this drug is that it can interfere with the breathing reflex. So Squeakers' seizures stopped with the drug, but she also nearly stopped breathing. Squeakers was quickly taken off Propafol.

"Because of the holidays we didn't have blood work back, and when we finally got it back two days later, her calcium was really low. There aren't many reasons to have a low calcium in a cat—antifreeze ingestion is one but she wasn't in kidney failure, which she should have been. So we figured she had an acute pancreatitis [inflammation of the pancreas]." After questioning the owner further, she reported that Squeakers had been writhing in pain before the seizures started, and she was vomiting profusely.

A healthy pancreas won't appear on ultrasound, but an inflamed one will.

"There was a radiology resident just walking through, and

I said, 'Can you ultrasound her quick?' She thought she had pancreatitis as well. At the time she thought she identified a big vessel," but the resident had just started, and she was not sure of her diagnosis.

Nonetheless, Terry treated her for pancreatitis, and Squeakers got better. "We thought that her neurologic signs—the seizuring activity—could be attributed to her calcium being so low. So she went home, and she did well for about a month."

But then at Christmas time, the owner called to say that Squeakers was having seizures again. The young man, in his twenties, lives far away at the tip of Cape Cod, and came the following week, the first of the new year, with Squeakers.

"So I had the cat here, and once again I'm thinking, I wonder if she's got a liver shunt because she's just acting weird, you know—a little drooly and acting encephalopathic." If the liver isn't functioning properly, and it isn't detoxifying naturally occurring ammonia, the ammonia can go to the brain and cause damage. "So once again I check the calcium, and it was normal this time, only now her ammonia was higher." Another ultrasound of her abdomen was taken. But because the owner was young and did not have much money, Terri performed a "quick peek" ultrasound—a fast look without the expensive full process that is filmed.

"So now they see a liver shunt." As we have seen, in this case the abdominal vessel "shunts" blood around the liver, so it cannot be detoxified.

Kittens are born with these shunts, which shut themselves down over time. The liver shunt Squeakers had was an acquired one—it had opened up after she had become an adult cat.

"Squeakers had an ammonia count that was really high. Normal is less than thirty and Squeakers was like five hundred. So she was like shunting through this vessel like crazy."

Squeakers was sent home for a short time with plans to

bring her in for surgery. The abnormal vessel would be tied off with a surgical suture.

"You hope that the cat's not too old because sometimes, if the liver hasn't gotten a good blood supply over time, it won't come back and sometimes when you try to ligate this, there's too much pressure and the liver can't take all this new blood, so there's backflow and the gut dies."

When Squeakers arrived the next week for her surgery, she was "more encephalopathic than ever," Terri says. "She was barely in this world. She was in a fog, just drooling." Ironically, in the state she was in, she was too ill for the surgery.

"Clearly, she was not a good candidate for surgery," Terri says. "Her ammonia was seven hundred at that point. Really high."

Terri had to get that ammonia level down, so she stepped up treatment for the hepatic encephalopathy using oral antibiotics and high-sugar syrup.

Quickly, Squeakers began to feel better. She didn't need to stay in the closely monitored ICU, and she was moved back to "B ward" with the other healthier patients. Her appetite was back and she appeared to be a happy cat.

But her condition suddenly went downhill again. She started twitching without any letup, a situation known as "in status." That means an animal is either experiencing seizures for more than twenty minutes at a time, or having seizures so frequently that the brain doesn't have time to recover between bouts. "And she was 'in status' for a couple of days," Terri explains, because early on no one recognized the minor, subtle twitches as seizures.

Terri was in a terrible bind. The sick cat needed to get better before she could have that vital surgery. Further complicating things, the drugs normally used to help stop seizures are metabolized by the liver. And Squeakers' liver was out of commission.

Terri recalls standing in the middle of the ICU during the

ordeal. "I must have checked it four times, and it's below analyzer range [below detection in blood work] every time. Finally, on the fourth one, the tech says to me, Terri, I think
we've got to trust it, it's below analyzer range. And I couldn't
stop her seizures."

Terri explains the chemistry of seizures. "You've got excitatory tone, which is when you function to remember something, to speak, to move, to do anything, you need neurons
that are called excitatory. They have excitatory function. And
then, you've got inhibitory function, which basically counter-
acts all of that. And so when you have too much inhibitory
tone, you have an excess of a neurotransmitter called GABA
[gamma aminobutyric acid]. Animals and people that are encephalopathic have too much inhibitory tone so usually they're
very comatosed or somnolent. They're in a fog."

Terri realize that she had treated Squeakers' brain chemistry as though she were a normal cat, and apparently she
was not.

"Squeakers must have been functioning for years with excess inhibitory tone, and here I thought I was correcting her
encephalopathy. I must have brought it down too acutely for
her to handle." This hunch was further confirmed when the
owner came in and said Squeakers looked better now than
ever before. "What I never really appreciated was that she
was probably encephalopathic all her life." The more Terri
spoke to him, "the more I realized that from day one she was
probably very sick."

As soon as Squeakers stopped having seizures, Terri
rushed her off to surgery. But nothing would go smoothly for
Squeakers. There were yet more problems in store.

When the surgeon opened Squeakers up, she found that
the pressure inside the shunt was too great to tie off the vessel
safely. "The pressure in there should be ten to fifteen," Terri
says. It shouldn't go up much over twenty when you tie off
the shunt." Yet when they put a ligature on her shunt, the

pressure went up over fifty. "So they undid the ligature, and they put on a really loose ligature that would slide up and down along the shunt." The pressure still went up to thirty, but they left it in place. They hoped that scar tissue would form over the shunt and close it a little bit. Then they would go in and do it again.

Between January and May, the little cat improved—ever so slowly, in tiny increments. Not until the end of spring could she get up on her own.

Then she took a turn for the worse. For two weeks in July, she experienced horrible seizures. It happened to occur while Terri was away taking exams. The vets operated again to close the shunt. This time the surgeon tried a constrictor ring—a device that would allow the shunt to close gradually on its own over the course of a few months.

At present, the operation seems to be successful. Since August, Squeakers has not needed any medication for the encephalopathy. But those nonstop seizures took their toll. Terri says, "It's only been in the last couple of months that she can get up on her own, stand on her own."

It is highly unorthodox, but Terri is caring for Squeakers until her owner feels he can take her back. The cat had only three legs to begin with, but Terri says, "She likes to putter here to here to here." Squeakers does have to take anticonvulsants, and "she's just a real battle because she's been brain injured from her seizures," Terri says. "She sat in B ward having seizures and if you look at the record, it's 'twitching, twitching, twitching,' but nobody recognized that the twitching was caused by her seizures. She wasn't lying on her side, exhibiting symptoms doctors commonly recognize."

Yet a question needs to be asked. After all that medicine, surgery, and effort, does Squeakers have a chance at a normal cat life? Terri has pushed the envelope too far as some are concerned. "The animal rights committee got upset with me," Terri says, "because they thought that it was cruel."

She disagrees. She sees in Squeakers a cat who is fighting to survive. The cat has made progress, and now she wants to do things on her own. "She's trying to figure out how to get up, and if I pick her up at home, she screams at me." She's now eating on her own. For a half year, Terri fed her food by syringe. "Then, for six months, I'd hold her on my lap and hold the food bowl, and guide her to eat it. And now I just put the food in front of her and she eats it." For a long time the food had to have the consistency of baby food for Squeakers to manage. But recently she has been able to eat soft canned food that is sliced up for her.

"In her mind there's nothing wrong with her," Terri says. "When I walk in the room at home, Squeakers looks in my direction more than my other cats do! And when I say, 'Who wants cat food?' Squeakers is the one that's squeaking for food.

"And when I walk in a room and when I say, 'Hi, everybody,' the one that's clamoring to get out to come see me is Squeakers. To me she's a very acceptable pet, and I hope she goes home because that's the whole point of it."

The what-ifs are many in her case. Terri says, "It's really too bad that somebody didn't identify her liver shunt when she was a kitten because she would have been fixed and been a normal cat."

Squeakers has been beating the odds from the beginning.

Her owner had heard about a litter of kittens about to be put to sleep at the local shelter, Terri says. He dashed down there to get one. When he arrived, the shelter workers told him he was mistaken. The kittens were going to be put up for adoption, not euthanized.

Almost as an afterthought, though, they said, "except for one," and they pointed to a tiny three-legged kitten. According to Terri, the owner replied, without hesitation, "No, you're mistaken—that's the one I want." And Squeakers began her odyssey.

THE HEART OF THE ICU

WHEN we conjure up an image of the ICU, most likely we see the frantic "code blue" scenario in our minds—the frightful excitement of cardiac arrest followed by frantic activity and the restoration of life in what was momentarily a lifeless body.

The harsh reality is that hardly any animal patients who reach this deadly state survive. Very few come back to life on the table. And of those, only a miniscule number do well enough to ever leave the hospital. It is estimated that fewer than 5 percent go back home; realistically, it may even be 1 to 2 percent.

But doctors continue to hope against hope that this patient, the one whose heart is lying motionless in the palms of their skilled hands, will surge back into the world of the living.

There are two kinds of resuscitation situations: pulmonary, in which the animal stops breathing but still has a heartbeat and pulse; and cardiac arrest, in which there is no heartbeat or pulse. Sometimes *external compressions* will do the trick. Pressing palms down rhythmically over the chest, the vet may get the animal's heart jump-started. Sometimes a *defibrillator* is used externally—jolting the chest with electrical currents. In humans, this is used to revive the heart, but not so with dogs. In helping canine patients, the defibrillator stops chaotic electrical activity within the heart so that doctors can then jump-start the heart chemically with epinephrine. In the most extreme cases, the chest cavity is cut open and the heart is massaged by hand and then jolted with the paddles of the defibrillator.

In his book, *Veterinary Emergency Medicine Secrets*, Wayne Wingfield says that CPR is "a desperate effort that helps only a limited number of patients. For most, CPR is unsuccessful."

Ask any vet in the ICU, and they'll tell you it's true. Dr. Lisa Powell says she has never had a patient survive cardiac resuscitation. She's never even witnessed such a success. Other vets may have experienced one or two CPR victories, and they are, without fail, vivid memories for them.

At Tufts, the situation is not called a code blue, though codes are posted on the cages of pets who are likely to experience such a sudden decline. Red means nothing is to be done to save the animal if the heart stops beating. Yellow means intubate (provide oxygen directly to the lungs by inserting a tube into the airway) and take other moderately invasive measures, but do not open chest. Green means "Go"—do everything, including opening the chest, to resuscitate.

Sometimes there is no color code at all, because no one suspected the patient would collapse.

Travis was such a case.

It is a lazy Sunday afternoon, and Ann Marie Crowninshield has no idea that her lovely gentleman of a German shepherd, Travis, will be the center of a frightening medical rescue attempt. He seems sick, but certainly not at death's door. At home, he hadn't been quite himself and his owner noticed that his abdomen was sensitive.

Her big, dark shepherd is wheeled back into the ICU on a

stainless steel gurney just before three o'clock. In a strange environment, being carted around on an odd contraption, Travis is either too polite or too sick to object. He lies quietly on the cold surface, blinking at those around him under the bright lights.

Dr. Lisa Powell is on duty but not admitting patients. She happens by Travis before the resident who will examine him gets there, so she checks him out. She takes a rectal temp, which is normal—100.9. His heart rate is normal—112.

She slips on a pair of powdery latex gloves for a rectal exam, saying, "Sorry, buddy," as she proceeds to violate his privacy. "Hmmm," Lisa says as she discovers a very lumpy prostate. She turns to a technician, "Bolus him a liter of fluids, please."

Just then Steve Mensack, on admitting duty, arrives at the gurney. Tall and thin, with a shaved head, goatee, and wearing two silver loop earrings in one ear, Steve is hipper than your average vet. He's wearing blue jeans with his white lab coat. Having just quit chewing tobacco, and being a bundle of energy anyway, Steve is always chomping a big wad of bubble gum.

Steve looks inside Travis's mouth, where the mucous membranes tell a great deal about an animal's health. Travis's gums are darkly pigmented and therefore hard to read, but his tongue is nearly brown. That could suggest a lack of oxygen.

Steve begins to shave Travis's abdomen as a technician holds flexible tubing that delivers oxygen to the dog's nose. An abdominal tap—inserting a needle to aspirate fluid—may help reveal what's going on. Blood would mean internal bleeding. Pus-like fluid could indicate sepsis, an invasion of bacteria. After swabbing the skin with alcohol, Steve strategically inserts two needles. "It works better on a tap than one, but we don't know why," he says. After the needles are inserted, the syringe portions are attached. Nothing seems to be coming out, so the needles are twirled and manipulated in new locations. Still nothing, but the syringes are pumped onto slides anyway, making sounds like small gasps and puffing a ghost of moisture onto each small clear square of glass. Steve says sometimes telltale cells have been drawn, even though you can't see anything with the naked eye.

Duffy, a fourth-year student who has spoken to Travis's owner and taken a preliminary history, goes over the dog's story with Steve. He begins with a little lingo.

"German shepherd. 'Ninety-one model. Intact male," Duffy says. Travis apparently began vomiting Friday, and was given the boiled hamburger/rice mixture that owners of dogs with upset tummies know so well, but he vomited that, too. His regular vet put him on antibiotics, to no avail—he was still vomiting this morning. He's been known to get into the trash, and he does eat cat food when he gets the chance.

Steve notes that Travis's prostate is large and firm on the left side, indicating some kind of tumor. At the other end, his right mandibular region, or jaw, is a bit enlarged. As for the body condition, Travis is a little thin.

Travis's issues right now are a painful abdomen, vomiting, and diarrhea. Diagnoses under consideration: gastritis, or inflamed gastric intestinal area; a foreign body lodged somewhere along the gastrointestinal tract; inflammatory bowel disease; obstruction; peritonitis; and given the detail of his eating cat food, which is high in protein and fat, perhaps pancreatitis.

There are lots of possibilities to choose from, so it's time for tests: blood work such as a CBC profile, the big four, blood gases. Also a urinalysis, X rays, and ultrasound. In the meantime, Steve wants to get fluids into him and "lytes," or electrolytes. The dog has been throwing up, and he needs fluids to get hydrated and also some electrolytes to keep his chemistry in balance.

"Let's put him in a run while we talk to his mom and dad," Steve says.

On the way to the examining room to talk to Travis's owner, Steve and Duffy stain the slides purple and look at the abdominal cells under a microscope. Nothing much shows up, nothing to give them a hint.

At a quarter to four, Steve meets Ann Marie. With dark shoulder-length hair and a fresh, nearly starched-looking sweatshirt, Ann Marie talks about Travis. She is concerned but not anxious. Steve asks her when she feels "Travis was last Travis," meaning his normal healthy self.

Tuesday, she says. It wasn't until Friday, though, that he stopped eating. That night he had a bout of diarrhea. On Saturday, that worsened and he suffered through several episodes of diarrhea. This morning, he vomited more, only this time it was a bilious bright yellow. And he seemed so weak. Her brother had to help Travis down the stairs and into the car to come to Tufts.

Any change in bathroom habits in general?

Actually, Ann Marie says, there had been some blood in his urine a month ago, but not since. For the past month, he had been getting into trash and the cat food more frequently, but otherwise he was a very healthy dog.

Steve updates her on what they found on initial examination. "We can make a few stories for causes," he says. He goes over the possibilities, citing the blood work and tests that need to be done. Certain problems would be apparent right away, Steve tells her. If Travis swallowed something from the trash that got stuck, it might show up on the X ray, for instance, or perhaps on ultrasound. "Right now, though," Steve tells her, "I can't tell you whether the solution is going to be medical or surgical." If it's a prostate problem, Travis will be treated and then neutered. An abscess would require surgery. "Obviously, we have to identify the cause before we can fix it," Steve tells Ann Marie. "I know I'm being vague right now, but we just don't have an obvious cause yet. Some of these are tough problems."

Steve is very straightforward. He believes softening the blow is a mistake. He outlines hospital policy and practice for Ann Marie: Visiting hours are between five p.m. and eight p.m. every day. Owners can call each morning and listen to a written update, which is read to them over the phone by an operator. Each afternoon a doctor—whichever one is handling the case at the time—will call in with current news.

Ann Marie has only one question after all this: How long will Travis have to stay in the hospital? Steve tells her the average stay is four days.

Ann Marie, who has seemed so confident and calm, now reveals that she is very worried about her poor dog. She has spent the last week sleeping downstairs in her house because Travis was unable to come upstairs. She is also concerned that he seems so thin.

She asks if she can come back to see him. It is a request she will later be happy she made.

When Ann Marie leaves the ICU after saying good-bye to Travis, Duffy wheels the dog to X ray. On the weekend most support staff members are off, so Duffy will run the X-ray equipment himself, weighed down by a bright blue lead apron. The apron is vital since vets or techs often must stay in the room during the process to position dogs and keep them still.

Travis, as sick as he is, still has perfect manners, accommodating all the positioning and manipulation. But he retches twice on the table when he is turned. Now his vomit is brown and granular, like coffee grounds—it is digested blood, caused by a stomach ulcer. Duffy gets pictures of the abdomen from the left and right, but trying to get another view, with Travis lying on his back, is too dicey. Since the dog is queasy from the slightest movement, there is too high a risk he will aspirate, or breathe some vomit into his lungs, which could cause aspiration pneumonia.

Like the slides under the microscope, the films are not conclusive. The axis of the stomach looks a little odd but not alarming. There is gas in the colon—air on an X ray shows up as black.

The intestines look fluidy but not distended (which would be consistent with obstruction). The liver looks a little small, the bladder big. "There's nothing that says surgery in this," Steve reports as he gazes up at the black and gray images on the light panel. It is just before five.

Travis is rolled back into ICU so he can relax in a cage, receive fluids and pain medication, and be still for a while. An ultrasound is planned for the next day. But before the run is even prepared, Travis goes into full cardiac arrest.

As the call goes out over the loudspeaker for Dr. Mensack to come to ICU stat, all hands go on deck. Six veterinarians and six students and techs surround the dying dog. Lisa Powell starts pumping Travis's chest like mad and calling for atropine—one of the important ingredients on a crash cart, it speeds up a slow heart rate.

Steve races in and takes over the pumping. He leaps onto the gurney, kneeling alongside Travis's lifeless body, and with both hands he begins pumping the chest rhythmically, one palm on top of the back of his other hand.

Everywhere are hands: connecting bags of fluid, taking blood samples, feeling for a pulse.

Crystalloid fluids are given to increase blood volume. These fluids are balanced and have electrolyte levels similar to that of blood. Nutrients like potassium, sodium, chloride, and calcium are vital to nerve and muscle function, and for retaining water.

The dog is not only given oxygen, but someone works an "ambu" or rebreathing bag, which acts like a bellows, pushing the lungs open for better volume.

All hands lift Travis's body up to put paper down underneath him on the gurney. This will stop the conduction of some of the electrical impulses from the defibrillator to the metal gurney, which could shock those around it. As soon as that's done, one vet passes Steve the electrical defibrillating paddles. Because he is the vet in charge, he shouts for everyone to get clear of the dog.

Everyone moves back, arms raised to show he or she is clear. This device can kill as well as save. Steve once worked with a young doctor who shocked the patient and *then* yelled clear. Steve was caught unaware and remembers his arms going completely numb.

The paddles deliver one jolt, then another, then a third.

Nothing.

Travis needs so many fluids, two catheter sites are set up. A back leg is being shaved for one. A slit is cut in his neck for another. In shock, Travis's blood pressure is extremely low, which collapses his veins. The cut in the neck with a scalpel will allow the team to see a jugular vein in which to place a catheter. It's called a *cut down*. The floor is now littered with syringe caps.

Blood samples are constantly being taken to check on glucose and blood-gas levels. The less oxygen to the tissues, the higher in acid it becomes. Travis's chest is being shaved. Quickly, Steve cuts the chest open behind Travis's front left leg, and in his rush he accidentally nicks the hand of another vet who is assisting. Everyone gasps. "It's just a flesh wound," she says with a laugh.

Steve reaches into Travis's chest, well past his wrists, and massages the great dog's heart. "How does his heart feel?" one doctor asks.

"Good," Steve replies, "good volume."

He places the paddles right on the heart itself and yells, "Clear!" Everyone recoils from the body, and another jolt is delivered. Steve removes the yellow paddles, which have become covered in blood.

It is 5:20. The paddles are applied two more times. Each time there is a dull thud followed by a jump from the dog's body.

Steve puts his hand in the chest. "We've got something now!" he shouts. Travis's heart is beating. Everyone is amazed. "Oh, great," someone cracks, "now we'll have to make a plan!" Everyone laughs.

Rocket, a three-legged greyhound who is housed in the run just inches from the action, and who has been lethargic, suddenly springs up with all the commotion. "Jeez, even Rocket's up!" someone yells. "Right," a technician responds. "Rocket's saying, 'I'm up! I'm up! Don't cut me open!' "

Relief, joy, amazement, pride, fill the ICU. It is 5:25 and Travis is alive. Epinephrine is continuously pumped into his system via IV to help stimulate the heart to keep beating.

"I guess you can start on the discharge orders, Lisa," one vet jokes.

A fourth-year student who has worked as a tech for many years says, "This is a victory. The dog's chances of leaving the hospital may be slim. But, man, this is a victory."

But within ten minutes of the victory, bad news. Steve, still standing over Travis, says, "Awww, he's slowing down." Several injections of epinephrine have been given over the long struggle. Travis's heart is still beating, but it's not strong and it's not regular. Grim-faced, the twelve people who have just been through this drama stop and stare. There's nothing more to do.

Five minutes later, Travis's heart gives out. He almost made it. But after the punishing, brutal efforts to save him, it's time to give up. In typically terse fashion, Steve says, "I think we're done here."

Silently, robotically, everyone begins the cleanup. Code blues may make great television, but in real life they're events no one relishes.

* * *

The staggering odds against these animals are hard for new vets to bear. Dr. Nishi Dhupa takes a philosophical view of the situation.

"When you're training residents, some of them are discouraged by this. When I talk to them, I try to emphasize that the animal is actually dead when its heart stops. They say within ten to fifteen seconds your brain is so deprived of oxygen that the cells begin to die, so really it's over and you're resuscitating a dead patient. So two to three percent is not bad, you know. If you look at it in those terms, that you're bringing a dead animal back to life, it's not bad at all."

The problem is that even if the animal comes through the frantic resuscitative crisis, it can be so damaged from the event that it never leaves the hospital. Care for a patient who is revived doesn't stop when the heart starts beating again. Some of the most critical care they receive is after all the excitement is over, when the body, so battered, struggles to recover.

"Your primary concern" with CPR, Nick Dodman says, "is to get things started again, but then immediately—almost simultaneously—you're thinking about the post-cardiac neurological deterioration problem. So neuro protection is what you're trying to provide, and there are some drugs that people think can help to prevent what can be irreversible neural damage."

"We do struggle a lot with what they call the post-resuscitation phase," Nishi says. "Even if you can make the heart beat and get the blood pressure going, the brain is affected by the hypoxia, or low oxygen level. It's damaged. And the damage is like a little cascade—it keeps going. It keeps going, and that's where we lose the battle. You get patients whose hearts and brains come back, and then they develop brain edema, or swelling. And their hearts slow down and they stop breathing and they slowly fade away. So you usually have to put them on a ventilator, use special drugs to protect their brains, and get the edema out of their brains." All of this, she notes, requires "very intensive care for that twenty-four hours at least, and that's where people fall down."

Owners can become panic-stricken at this point. They are asked to commit a lot of money to save a pet who may not make it or live in a very diminished capacity—blind or not able to walk normally.

"Often owners give up at that point," Nishi says. "And you have to say to them, you need to commit to twenty-four hours on the ventilator and unfortunately, it will cost you so much money, and we can't tell you what the outcome will be because your dog could be brain dead when we try to wake it up. It could be anywhere from brain dead to slightly blind." Sometimes the blindness is only temporary. "That's almost the best-case scenario. And so that doesn't sound too good."

Survivors of this scenario are so rare that if one is successful, a buzz goes around the hospital. Everyone was bragging one day in February about a blue merle collie who beat the odds.

Dr. Maureen McMichael covered the case. It was thought to be a "toxicity," the kind of case Maureen is skilled in. But the dog was not responding to treatment, and the doctors began to suspect a neurological problem—a brain tumor perhaps.

The owners were asked if they wanted a CAT scan for the dog. "They decided to go with it," Maureen says, "but during the CAT scan, he arrested and he really died. His heart stopped. We had to defibrillate him. But they got him back and they put him on the ventilator for a day because he wasn't breathing appropriately, and now he's walking." The collie did go home, diagnosed with a toxic reaction to an antiparasite drug.

All of the vets remember resuscitations from the past that have worked. There are so few and they are so exciting, they always tell you a vivid tale.

Dr. Gretchen Schoeffler remembers a terrier named Bravo who came in one night while she was working as an intern at the University of Georgia. "As an intern you typically have one or two cases that are your big cases," Gretchen says. "Well, Bravo was my big case."

"He came in to me late at night, probably about eleven o'clock, and he had been the victim of his house mate. Another dog he'd been living with for three or four years attacked him."

Bravo belonged to a couple slated to be married in two weeks. "The big dog was his and the little dog was hers," Gretchen says. Most days the two dogs were left outside in the fenced-in backyard while the owners went to work. From information Gretchen could patch together, the two apparently got into a fight and the big dog tore the little terrier to pieces. It most likely happened first thing in the morning, probably about nine. Neighbors later reported that they thought they heard something going on at the time.

Wounded severely and losing blood, Bravo, a true terrier, fought to survive. Probably running on pure adrenaline, he dug his way to safety under the fence. After that he hid out, somehow staying alive.

The owners found him around two o'clock and brought Bravo to their regular vet. He was bandaged up and stabilized there and finally, when fit enough to endure the ride, sent to the ICU at the University of Georgia. The owner carried the dog back into the ICU, against all rules of the hospital.

"I was a little perturbed, you know," Gretchen says, laughing at herself now, "because you have the owner there, and you're an intern anyway, you don't want your insecurities showing or what not." The owner looked at her and said, "He's a very special dog." Gretchen replied, "You have to go back up front," and brought the paperwork along.

A soft-tissue surgeon happened to still be in the hospital late that night, and he popped his head in to check on the young intern. "I said, 'Can you look at this with me? It looks pretty bad,' " Gretchen recalls. "We got the dog, started to undo the bandage, and we realized that this was going to be a major ordeal. And so we called in Dr. Quandt, who was the anesthesiologist, to come in and anesthetize him for surgery to explore the wound."

For stable emergencies late at night, the intern or resident can put the animal under anesthesia on her own. For major surgery, an anesthesiologist must put the animal in a deep sleep. The anesthesiologist's knowledge comes in handy as critical patients can decline rapidly. Keeping a patient sedated is a complicated art and science, and requires someone's full attention.

Gretchen laughs and says that to this day, Dr. Quandt teases her and says that over the phone she downplayed the horror of Bravo's injuries. She described the little dog's problem as a "little neck laceration."

"She couldn't imagine why I needed her to come anesthetize the dog for a little neck laceration," Gretchen says.

The anesthesiologist found out.

"As she tells it, when she got there, she realized the dog had a partial *decapitation*! Literally, his whole neck was ripped out. He was like an anatomy specimen. We had him on his back, and the arteries and the veins were suspended. There was no muscle left.

"His trachea was ripped open, and when I was lavaging and cleaning things out with saline, as I ran my fingers under his trachea, along his neck, the bones—his vertebrae— penetrated my gloves," she says. "All the muscles that protect the neck were gone."

The complications of the surgery were compounded by another problem. "He had so much blood and dirt go down his airway because his airway had been ripped open, and then he had dug his way out of the yard. So, there was dirt all down in his wound that had tracked down through his neck into his mediastinum. We performed a tracheostomy [cutting an opening to the trachea through the neck] that night and cleaned the wound as best we could. For several days he was anesthetized, and bandage changes were performed three times a day." Over the course of his hospital stay, Bravo continued to cough up foreign matter, which intermittently blocked his tracheostomy site—"popping up and down his airway like a pea in a pipe. And one time I caught some. I could see some coming up, and I took a pair of forceps and I caught it and yanked it out."

During his month-long hospitalization, Bravo's heart stopped beating on three separate occasions. Each time Gretchen performed external compressions to jump-start the organ. "We got him back every time," she reports happily, "and he went home. The couple were married two weeks later, and they moved to the Philippines. The husband made a large donation to the University of Georgia. That was over and above the bill for Bravo's care, which was more than $10,000.

"I still get e-mails from the Philippines every once in a while from Vivian and her husband. Bravo has a permanent tracheostomy now, and they keep it covered over so the mosquitos don't find his little trach site when he goes outside. They have two other dogs. The maid takes care of Bravo and holds his food bowl for him. And the gardener takes him to the tennis courts every day and throws the ball for all the dogs.

"Vivian was right about Bravo being a special dog," Gretchen says. "The dog never once bared a tooth. Never growled. All the things that we did to that dog, he was the best patient. He knew we were trying to help him. He was a good dog."

In an arrest, everyone runs to the scene, and the doctor whose patient is dying is like the captain of a team. Gretchen says of orchestrating a resuscitation effort in a big teaching hospital, "It's more difficult here than in private practice. In private practice where you have the same people there pretty much day in and day out, you actually get a very good team effort going in, everybody knows their job.

"Here it's more difficult because we have different students all the time. We've had a high turnover in technical support as well. And there's different doctors around and everybody does things differently.

"You learn real quickly not to say, 'Somebody do this or that.' You have to point a finger and say, 'Hey, you!'—if you don't know the name—'I need two milliliters of epinephrine,' or whatever you want. Sometimes the arrests go real smoothly and you feel like it was a good effort, sometimes they don't. I don't know if it makes a difference in the long run because most of them don't make it, but certainly you feel a lot better when it's gone smoothly."

A good team effort is important during the frantic, split-second action. "Most of the time," Gretchen says, "there will be somebody who's got more knowledge than you do, and they'll make a suggestion if they think that there's something else that should be done or could be done. Some are better at letting you find your own way and make the decisions. Others jump in and kind of take over."

Gretchen says she's done that herself. "I always tell people you can't have soft feelings in an arrest. People are going to bark things at you, and it's not that anybody is being mean or that you're doing anything wrong. It's just a high-tension situation where seconds count."

Ultimately, the chances of bringing an animal back to life are so slim that a vet would have a hard time feeling that he blew it. "In an arrest situation it's a no-lose situation—the patient is dead. You can only be a hero. You can't mess up."

Animals requiring resuscitation are not always in cardiac arrest. Sometimes, they are in real danger of dying because they are in shock, either from loss of blood or septic shock, in which the body is overwhelmed by a raging bacteria.

For these problems, emergency medicine recently has taken a quantum leap forward with the advent of new products that have allowed doctors to save patients who would certainly have died a decade ago. These new "resuscitative fluids" actually pour life back into dying animals. They may be synthetics, but they actually work better and faster than real blood or plasma.

"We have these synthetic colloids that are like plasma, and we almost invariably save ninety percent of the patients that would have died a decade ago," says Nishi Dhupa.

She points to animals who have "bled out" and are in severe shock. Not long ago, she says, you couldn't "retrieve them" when they had gone that far. With shock, the entire system collapses. Blood carrying oxygen doesn't reach the organs, and cellular waste materials build up to toxic levels. "You get to a certain point where the organs are so compromised that they begin to fail." Today, vets are able to "pull them back."

The synthetic plasmas, she says, "are really powerful agents. You can bolus them into a patient and very, very rapidly raise blood pressure, which helps deliver oxygen to the organs. So whereas before it would take you an hour, you can now raise blood pressure in a matter of minutes. And so you have bought yourself that huge period of time."

These materials were in their infancy in human medicine when veterinary ICUs started using them in earnest.

"We jumped on the bandwagon in veterinary medicine really early on," Nishi says. "And in fact there was more use of them in veterinary ICUs than there was in human medicine for the longest time. Even now I think if you read about resuscitation in human medicine, we are still probably using those agents more. But the success rate is phenomenal."

It's hard to imagine that a bag of fluids could be as important as a defibrillator in the ICU, but it is. "Whenever you re-suscitate a patient, you're trying to resuscitate them from a shock situation," Nishi explains. "The definition of shock in its most simple sense is that there's a lack of oxygen to tissues. That's because of the low blood pressure. So what you want to do is increase the pressure and deliver oxygen. The hall-marks of shock therapy are oxygen supplementation and fluids . . . and the quicker you can give them fluids and the better those fluids are at staying in the blood vessels and maintaining blood pressure, the quicker you will resuscitate. That really is the essence of it."

Nick Dodman remembers an incredible resuscitation that proves two points: you never know what the outcome will be in such cases, and no good deed goes unpunished.

"I walked into what they call the induction room, which is where they knock them out, anesthetize them, and then they go to the surgery rooms," he recalls. "I saw this cat lying on a table dead. It wasn't breathing and its pupils were dilated."

He asked the techs washing instruments after the surgery, "What happened to the cat?" "Cardiac arrest," he was told.

"Anybody tried to resuscitate it?"

"Yeah, we tried for a few minutes, but it's hopeless."

"Well, you know, I think I'll try."

Nick grabbed some equipment and went to work. "I lifted the cat's head on my own, I put a tube down its windpipe, at-tached it to the T piece circuit [one end of a piece of anes-thesia equipment], and put my finger at the end of the T piece so I could inflate its lungs. I put my other hand around its chest and squeezed." He massaged its heart, ventilating its lungs, not really expecting anything to happen. "Maybe I was sort of secretly hoping for a miracle."

The next thing he knew the heart was beating. "The heart—it had been dead for five minutes!—so the heart starts beating—*boom, boom, boom, boom.* I said, 'The heart's beating!' " They were not impressed. Anyone who has taken a physiology class knows that a frog's heart can be detached and placed in a bowl of saline. It will continue to contract on its own, but it's not a sign of life. It's just a reflex. In those cases, the heart is doing on its own what is called *idioventricular rhythm.*

Nick proceeded to dress this cat up and put on ECG electrodes. Looking at an ECG monitor, he saw a normal-looking trace. "I decided to stop ventilating him and see whether he could take a breath on his own. There was a long pause, but then . . . a breath! And then another one. Now the heart was beating, and the cat was breathing pure oxygen on his own."

Everyone began to take note. "Clearly, there had been some kind of physiological recovery. And even the pupil size started to come down a little bit, it seemed to me. We put him on a heating pad."

Nick had just been passing through. He had a lot to do that day. But you don't just walk away from a miracle.

"I probably stood with him for about an hour, and he actually started to arouse in a groggy kind of way—trying to raise his head. And we took him through to a nice warm spot."

Nick was feeling a bit like a hero, for he had brought someone's beloved cat back from the dead. "I thought people were going to say to me, 'Boy, that's amazing, you know, this is the Lazarus get-up-from-your-deathbed-and-walk scenario. This cat was dead and now it's alive, it's a miracle!' But instead people said, 'That's disgraceful what you just did. This cat will have brain damage, it will be a vegetable, you should have just let it go.' "

The cat did recover the next day, but he had two problems. He was blind, and he had a drunken ataxic gait. Nick's critics said, I told you so.

But Nick really had pulled the cat out of the bag. "One

week later he wasn't blind, he walked well and he went home."

Nick also had a more unusual case come his way a few years ago. "I remember a professor of surgery at the time gave an overdose of anesthetic to a cat." There were two barbiturates of different strengths: one was 2.5 percent and one was 5 percent. "We were supposed to use the 2.5 percent on cats. He pulled the wrong bottle by mistake. Pulled 5 percent pentathal and injected the usual volume."

With the doubled dose, the frail old cat's heart stopped, its respiration stopped. The panicked doctor shouted for help, and Nick came over from the other side of the room.

"I put the tube down its throat," he recalls, "and I started to breathe for the cat and massage its heart." He did manage to get the heart beating again, but the cat still wasn't breathing. "Every time I stopped, its color [determined by its gums, nose, and eye area] started to deteriorate, and I had to keep breathing for it."

Someone shouted out a suggestion. Nick had been interested in acupuncture, and the tech said, "Why don't you try this particular point on the nose? You know, you were telling us about how you'd read about it." "So I put the needle directly in there and started to twist it and peck it backward and forward in the nose. Then Morgan Long, who was a student and really an electric whiz, came along," he says. He had a small electrical generator. The two hooked the generator up to needles at points in the nose and the paw for what is called electro acupuncture.

They turned the current up to a point that they could see some mild circulation. The cat started to breathe on his own, his pupils contracted, and he made a good recovery.

"Everything came back. He was breathing. His color was good. His heart was beating stronger. And his blood pressure felt good."

Nick says the space age effort reminded him more of a *Star Trek* episode than a segment of *ER*. "It was almost like in the *Starship Enterprise*," Nick says, "when Dr. Bones comes and gives an injection," and the patient springs back to life.

MY, WHAT BIG TEETH YOU HAVE

THIS time the young veterinarian is prepared.

She is treating a dog with heart problems whom she saw for the first time weeks ago. The incident was one of the most hair-raising she'd ever had. Makita, the 102-pound rottweiler, made clear—suddenly and without warning—that she would not tolerate a medical examination. And when a massive rottweiler will not tolerate something, you'd better pay attention.

It had all started so pleasantly. In the waiting room before the exam, the young dog wore a benign expression. When she was spoken to, even by strangers, her little black stump of a tail shuttled back and forth with tremendous energy, enough to get her rump swaying. So when she first came to Tufts weeks ago, no one had any concern about treating her.

But from the moment a stethoscope was placed on her chest, the dog switched personalities. Her energy was directed not to the wagging tail but to a snarling frenzy. Everyone involved was shaken, but Makita was safely muzzled and no one was bitten.

Today, weeks later, the young vet and Makita meet again.

It's time for her recheck. As the big black dog enters the examining room, a strategy has already been mapped out to prevent anyone on staff from being attacked.

Dr. Armelle de Laforcade (pronounced *dee la fork ahd*) wants to get an EKG reading this afternoon. Makita's malformed valve and enlarged heart were discovered fortuitously by a vet at Tufts who heard an irregular heartbeat during a routine visit. At the time no none suspected a problem because Makita seemed the picture of health. She was perhaps a bit thin, but on the healthy side of underweight.

That discovery is saving Makita's life. The condition is significant, and though Makita will most likely not live out a normal life span, she can be treated for a good many years with medication. Without the diagnosis the dog might have suddenly collapsed and died at home without warning.

The problem now is that regular EKG monitoring is vital, and the dog's temperament makes a normal reading impossible. Anytime an animal fends off doctors with aggression, the care is diminished.

Armelle, tall and lanky, wearing a gray Cornell sweatshirt and jeans for this New Year's holiday weekend shift, explains the issues. If we sedate her for the EKG, we get a misleading reading, she says. If we don't sedate her—Armelle raises her eyebrows here—she'll go after us. Armelle has a healthy respect for the power of the dog, but she is not afraid to take the case on. To her it is a puzzle that needs to be worked out.

Muzzling Makita does work, but even with the muzzle she will thrash and struggle. Under these conditions, the solid, thick-muscled dog could still harm someone. Her muzzle could slip off. Furthermore, she would become so agitated that even if the alligator clips to the machine were somehow to miraculously stay on her, the reading, which maps out her heart rhythms, would be off the chart, and unusable.

Armelle has ruled out the use of tranquilizers—they'll only make the reading unreliable. Her best hope is that if the owner is present, he can keep her calm enough to complete the procedure. He has such faith in his own dog that he even brings in his young son. Still, the owner is asked to muzzle her as a precaution. Having never witnessed the aggressive behavior himself, the owner complies, but is skeptical that such restraint is needed.

As soon as the little alligator clips are applied to the elbows of her front legs and to the front of her thighs, Makita turns threatening. Her entire body goes rigid with hostility. She bristles. Everyone in the room can see the menacing change in her stance and attitude. There is no mistaking her mood or intent. She sizes up those closest to her. Everyone is shut in a room with a large agitated dog, who seems to have inflated herself to an even larger size.

Makita's eyes roll back as she begins to whine and struggle. The owner is shocked by the transformation. He puts his nose up to her muzzled one and speaks soothingly to her. "It's all right, girl, shhhh, shhhh." Makita does quiet some.

Armelle jumps at the chance, and quickly gets a reading from the machine. But because of Makita's movement, the jagged inked line on the long strip of paper is unusable. They have to try again. As they set up once more, placing the clips on Makita, the dog tenses but stays in a down position on the floor.

As stressful as this is, Armelle says to the owner, "This is a hundred times better with you here."

"I think she's just scared," he says.

"The only scary thing is you wouldn't know, meeting her," Armelle says as she prepares to take another reading. "Now we know."

With two more readouts, Armelle believes she has a strip from which she can calculate an accurate heart rate. Once again she discusses the prognosis with the owner, telling him, "There's no reason Makita can't live on for a good long time. She may not have any problems for years."

"I'm just ecstatic that she's not just going to suddenly die next week," the owner says, smiling down at the now angelic dog.

Outside the examining room, Armelle places the good reading down on a countertop and lays her pen parallel to it. This is a trick of the trade. The average pen length represents a duration of about three seconds on an EKG reading. Armelle notes the number of high points present for the length of the pen and then multiplies that figure by 20 to calculate the heart rate for one minute. Makita's rate a few weeks ago, before receiving medication, was 220. Today it is 160. It's a terrific improvement and not a bad reading: normal for a dog of this size is 100 to 120.

Armelle quickly consults with another ICU veterinarian, and they decide Makita is doing well enough to simply stay on her meds with a recheck in a month or two.

The owner is relieved to be taking his dog home, while Armelle is thankful just to be in one piece. Most physicians don't have patients who may maul, bite, scratch, hiss, trample, or spit. For veterinarians, especially those in the emergency room, it is a common occurrence.

Dr. Nick Dodman explains that when an animal is in pain, anything can happen. For just this reason, people whose dogs have been hit by cars are often warned to muzzle the injured animal if possible, even with a belt, before moving it.

Nick's wife, Linda, also a veterinarian, recently cared for a dog injured badly by a car. The poor dog was found lying on the road, whimpering in pain, and they suspected its back was broken. As Nick describes it, Linda "got in her car and sped down to the scene of the accident." As the dog was gently assisted onto a makeshift gurney, Linda warned those assisting her that dogs in pain frequently bite.

At the hospital, as the gurney was being carried up the stairs, it tilted. To prevent the dog from slipping off, Linda thrust her hand out reflexively to steady it. Wracked with pain, the dog bit down hard on the hand that appeared before his face.

"Everything that she had warned everyone about came true, and it went straight for her hand," Nick says. The dog's bite punctured the skin in several places, but missed the tendons and bone.

Though Nick was concerned for his wife, he is a man of science and can't help thinking about the chemical basis for such behavior. "It probably was a very fine dog under normal circumstances, but in pain," he says, "they release catecholamines, and catecholamines increase aggression."

This is essentially the fight or flight syndrome.

That state of aggressive arousal can last even after the crisis has passed. Dr. Lisa Powell, who has been bitten on the arm by a police dog, nabbed by a pit bull, and scratched by cats, remembers a close call recently with a German shepherd—ironically, an animal whose life she had just saved.

"The dog had a ball stuck in the back of his throat," she says, recalling the frantic emergency. The shepherd had been unable to breathe for quite a while, and he was near death by the time the owners got him to the clinic. Lisa and other ICU staff had a terrible time trying to dislodge the ball, which was wedged in tightly. Invasive measures would have to be taken if the problem wasn't fixed fast. "When we got the ball out, he was almost about to die. In fact, it looked like we were going to have to trach him [do an emergency tracheotomy to open an airway]. But we got it out." Lisa says there was a great celebration in the cramped quarters of the ICU over this very dramatic rescue.

When Lisa looked over at the rescued dog, though, she saw how stressful the ordeal had been for him. He was panting, and she figured his mouth must still be filled with saliva. She got him some water, and when she was reaching over to put it down, "he just looked up at me and went 'Ahhhrgghhh!' and snapped at me! But he only got my hair."

* * *

In the veterinary world, close calls abound.

One afternoon a call came back to the ICU that a very aggressive pit bull was out front. She had been hit by a car and needed to be examined. Matt, the biggest guy in ICU, happened to take the call. Reluctantly, he grabbed a soft muzzle and a blue vinyl leash.

At the front desk, a receptionist told him the pit bull was so aggressive, it was being kept out in the parking lot, far away from the other animals in the waiting room. More good news for Matt.

Striding out through the double set of glass doors in front, he found a brindle pit bull bitch standing with her tough-looking owner. As Matt approached, the black and brown dog lowered her head and growled menacingly. "I'm going to hand you the muzzle to slip on her," Matt told the man. With the muzzle on, and a leash clipped to her collar, Matt attempted to lead her in. But she threw her great bulk around in a thrashing frenzy, her bizarre movements like those of a marlin caught on a fishing line. The owner grabbed her and calmed her down, eventually handing the hostile dog off to Matt, who struggled to get her back to ICU.

Once inside, there were no clean cages immediately available, so Matt tied her to a cage door while he began to scrub it out. Suddenly, the pit bull began to thrash once again, heaving herself from side to side, and the muzzle, which the owner had not secured tightly, fell off.

The dog was bristling with rage and on the loose. Everyone froze in their tracks.

Val Kouloyan saw the incident from across the room, and quietly picked up another muzzle. Val is the head of the technicians and a model of understated competence. Speaking in soothing tones to the dog, she seamlessly slipped the muzzle over the animal's face and buckled the contraption in a heartbeat—a pounding heartbeat.

Once the pit bull was secure, Matt finished cleaning out the cage, and the dog was put in. No one talked about it afterward. They just went back about their business. It was all part of the job.

There is a famous case at Tufts, though, that makes that snarling pit bull in a closed room seem like a day at the park with a pampered pomeranian in comparison.

"It's like an episode of *When Animals Attack*. And it's not a very flattering story for me, I'm afraid, but it's the truth," Nick Dodman says as he sits in his quiet, sunny office, remembering the famed tale. "I had this young resident working with me at the time who had come over from Australia." Nick explains that in Great Britain and Australia, students can go right from high school into veterinary school, which is not the case in America. "Michael was very precocious," Nick says, "a smart guy, twenty-two years old."

This young doctor had served a year of his internship at Tufts, working with Nick, when the incident occurred. "He was just beginning to feel his own prowess at performing certain techniques," Nick says, "as you do as your specialist training goes on."

Into this scene stampeded an unusual patient, a castrated bull. "We don't very often do live bovines. It was about a thousand pounds, something like that," Nick says. "It definitely wasn't a poodle."

The animal was already being restrained in one of the large animal wards. "It was restrained in stanchions, which is very safe for us," Nick says. "It's like a big sort of metal caliper that comes together and holds the bull's head." With the bull safely secured, Michael proceeded to insert a needle catheter in its neck to deliver the anesthetics. "He put this big catheter in—it's about eight inches long and very fat, because you're injecting through the cow's skin, which is like leather." Nick pauses. "In fact, it is leather!" he says with a laugh. "It really is like injecting through a shoe."

The usual procedure is to make a nick in the skin with a scalpel, but the needle popped through, and he finally bent it in. They could see a vein, but Nick sensed that Michael had missed it.

Nevertheless, he continued, not realizing his mistake, and Nick was not positive he had witnessed one. Then, as is customary, the vet stitched the catheter in place onto the animal's skin with a surgical suture. That's when Nick voiced his concern. "I said, 'You know, Mike, I'm not sure that catheter went in.' And he said, 'I think it did.'"

The response was a little cocky.

That made Nick feel "a little bit naughty" himself, he says. Nick figured, "He's going to be anesthetizing animals in the middle of the night, he has to do whatever he has to do, and if he says it's in, we'll just let it go."

So Nick, the more experienced doctor, said nothing more, and the assembled surgical team moved on with their work. They led the big bull across the corridor and into what is called an *induction room*. The walls of these small rooms are padded, and a large, hinged board protrudes from the wall.

With big farm animals such as horses or cows, anesthetic is administered here. As the animal grows drowsy, the surgical team swings the squeeze board out and, all heaving together, they press the animal against the wall to steady it and guide its fall. When the animal slumps into unconsciousness, the drop is gentle and contained, and the animal doesn't hurt itself.

"Before we had moved it, we had given it a tiny bit of tranquilizer, Rompun, and it was a little bit sedated already." The bull was still standing, but his head was hanging low, in a blissful, mellow state.

The young Australian vet continued with the anesthetic procedures. First, they would be using a technique in which a strong muscle relaxant is administered, and once the animal shows some signs of going limp, an anesthetic is delivered as a chaser. "Then it falls to the ground," Nick explains.

"And then you intubate it." Using a metal shoehorn-like device, a tube is inserted into the airway, which is connected to a ventilator.

"Mike started that whole sequence, and he connected his drip with the muscle relaxant up to this suspicious catheter and started to infuse it," Nick says. If the needle was stuck in the tissues instead of the vein, Nick expected that it wouldn't run. But in fact it started to drip. High up in the line is a clear plastic vial, called *the drip chamber*, which gives visual confirmation of the fluid's progress and rate. Nick was surprised to see the liquid moving along. Maybe it had been inserted into the vein, after all.

Just then, though, the bull came to life in the tiny, sealed room. The animal shook off his drugged state, as a person would when fighting to stay awake while driving a car late at night. He lifted his head, waved it back and forth, blinked open his now alert eyes, mooed in an angered wail, and, as Nick says, he "crinked" his ears.

There was a full second's pause. Time froze. Then the enraged bull went crazy, knocking equipment over and popping the catheter right out of its muscular neck.

"We're all in this tiny room with this completely berserk bovine!" Nick says, with the particular delight of telling a scary story from the safe distance of time.

Ever the logical scientist, he realized what had happened. "It suddenly occurred to me," he says, "that this stuff actually stings when it goes around the vein. It's an irritant! And it woke him right up—into full, snorting bovine life!"

"I saw it happening in slow motion," Nick says. "I was knocking over women and children to get out!" Nick has a good laugh at his own expense. "I dove out the door! I thought, 'Every man for himself!' Everyone else came screaming after me, and we slammed the door shut, it was just like—*Boom*! Then we dropped this big bar in place." They all sighed with relief, having escaped an incredible danger.

"But then we turned to each other, and someone says, 'Hey where is Donnie?' And someone says, 'Where is Carl?' " Two members of the surgical team were not with them outside the room.

"There was a little glass portal and we looked in, and there they were, still inside with the bull! They were so scared, they had jumped up on top of this swing gate, and their faces were completely blanched white." Meanwhile, the huge animal "was doing the matador/bull thing—Boom! Boom! on the squeeze board!"

Nick says their expressions alone said, Get me out of here! "Oh, my God," Nick says, practically out of breath just reliving the wild moment.

"We did eventually manage to distract the steer while they fled out of some side door, but it wasn't without some considerable risk. The animal was still flailing, crazy mad and determined to kill anybody who came anywhere near it."

Being a full-service veterinary operation, they called in their wildlife vet at the time, Dr. Charles Sedgwick, who came and shot the animal several times with a tranquilizer gun.

Dodman was ribbed for his athletic feat of dashing out the door before everyone else. "What are you going to do?" he asked them. "The ground opens up, you just move." He says the others simply rolled their eyes and said, "Yeah, we noticed that."

When working with a big, unpredictable animal like a bull, the Tufts doctors know to be on their guard. But usually their dangerous patients are much smaller, and often cute as can be.

Dusty, a sixteen-year-old orange tabby, is clean and fluffy and wears a silver bell around her neck. The last few days, she has been lethargic, coughing a lot, and having occasional seizures.

A veterinary student has brought her inside her carrier into an examining room, while the owners remain in the waiting area. Gretchen Schoeffler, in a weathered green zippered sweatshirt and black jeans, enters the room. She cannot entice Dusty out of the carrier, so she upends the carrier slowly on the floor. When Gretchen goes to examine her, the old, sick, fragile cat transforms herself into a mountain lion. She raises her body up to full height, and with her hair standing up, she looks huge. Hissing and howling, she warns everyone to back off.

Gretchen sits on the floor, her back against the wall, ankles crossed. She says she's more comfortable sitting like that, but the fact is, she makes everyone else—owners and pets—relax by adopting that posture. To pets, she is low and therefore not as threatening. To owners, the veterinarian suddenly becomes a regular person, someone you can talk straight with. Time and again, Gretchen wins over pets and people.

Dusty takes refuge on the floor under the bench, and Gretchen notices that she is "ataxic in the hind," meaning that she starts to tip over in the rear as she crosses the room. She seems to have lost muscle mass in her thighs—which indicates that she hasn't been using her hind end in walking very much. Dusty walks back over to the carrier, but with the door shut and latched, she can't get in.

"I've learned the hard way always to make sure the carrier door is closed *and* locked," Gretchen says with a laugh.

After a few minutes, it is clear that Dusty is not settling down. So Gretchen gathers a thick, faded green cotton blanket and throws it over the reluctant patient. Screams and growls reverberate from under the doubled-up material. Gretchen unwinds the stethoscope from around her neck—all the vets wear their stethoscopes looped around their necks sidesaddle, with the listening device on one side of their chests and the ear plugs on the other. It's hard to hear anything useful through the barrier of the blanket and with all the fierce racket coming from underneath it. Gretchen tries to hold the squirming form still, but Dusty manages to hook a claw into her finger anyway.

"Ouch!" Gretchen says as she looks at a tiny gash on her middle finger. "And we're going to need blood work on her! Well, if worse comes to worst, we can always use Ketamine [a wildlife tranquilizer]."

Pets that refuse to be examined obviously cannot get the best care. Gretchen has the same problem with Dusty as Armelle had with the rottweiler. "I can't even do a physical exam," Gretchen says. "I think she has a neurological problem, and if I sedate her, I've totally messed up any ability to do a good neurologic exam. If she has a heart problem, I may kill her depending on what sedative I use."

When the owners come in, they go over her history. Dusty has had thyroid problems. Gretchen points out that her deteriorating health could signal heart or neurological problems. It is time-consuming and expensive to distinguish diagnostically between the two. For the owners, Dusty's age and her unhappiness with being examined weigh heavily. With sedation, she could have chest X rays, blood work, a cardiology exam, and even a CAT scan. But there is no quick fix.

"Realistically," Gretchen tells them, "this could get expensive." She leaves them alone to think it through. Minutes later, the husband says they are not prepared to spend thousands and make the cat miserable.

Gretchen tells him they could increase Dusty's thyroid medication, though that is unlikely to change much. "If you're prepared tonight to put Dusty to sleep," Gretchen says quietly, "we can do that. What I don't want to do is send you on some emotional roller coaster."

Dusty goes home that night, sick but peaceful in her carrier.

The vet's scratch is minor. Gretchen says she's lucky, she's really never been bitten. But when she starts to think about it, a few incidents pop up. "Actually, I was bitten by a rat once—

a lab rat," she says. "Oh, and also a kitten I was putting to sleep. It died with its teeth in my finger." After thinking a few seconds, she also remembers an English springer spaniel. "It had been really nice, and I was very caught off guard. It went for me, and it grabbed a watch like this, you know," she says grabbing onto her watch. "It ripped it off, threw it twenty feet, and shattered it against the wall across the room!"

Rose Borkowski is the exotics vet, which means she's been bitten and scratched by a wider variety of animals than the average vet. She says her record was pretty good for a long period of time. But she didn't have a technician for three years, and she believes the fatigue caught up to her. Every veterinarian, zoo worker, or anyone who deals with animals will tell you that fatigue is your worst enemy. "You have to be so careful. There is so little margin for error with these guys. It's very easy to hurt them," she says. Still, even when "you're dealing with a tiny little three-hundred-gram parrot, with that kind of mandible and beak they can really hurt you."

Rose remembers having a big caseload all summer long, and that's when she had a bad injury that kept her from working for weeks.

She was examining a pet parrot. As it struggled to get away, it managed to slip a sharp claw under the skin of Rose's middle finger. "It just injected bacteria when it poked me," she says. Animals have a lot of bacteria in their mouths, and their feet and nails can carry all kinds of things, including bits of feces. "I really didn't realize at the time what had happened, so I didn't stop and wash up right then. I had a lot of cases that day, and I just kept going and going. Then I realized my finger was infected." But with no other exotics vet to turn her cases over to, Rose kept working—into the middle of the next week. That's when the petite blonde's middle finger blew up to "the size of a frankfurter" and her lymph nodes became badly swollen. Whatever the germs were that traveled under her skin, they were strong. When an initial round of antibiotics failed, she had to go into the hospital for IV antibiotics.

Another time a parrot bit her, and again she didn't realize it right away—until she saw blood running down the bird's face and realized it was coming from her own hand.

Recently, she was bitten badly by an iguana. "I had a flap of skin hanging off my thumb. I did wash that one like crazy. She's a nice iguana, but she had finally gotten mad. We had X rayed her, and then we bled her from her tail [to collect a blood sample for testing]. We were pretty much done with her. I was just clipping her toenails, and I must have let my guard down.

"My tech was holding her, but I reached in front of her face. And she had been stressed. Sometimes when iguanas are stressed, they hold their breath and turn blue. Something must have happened in her little reptile brain while she was low on oxygen," Rose says. "This hand came in front of her and crunch! It sounded like potato chips being munched on."

One of Rose's worst bites came from a baby squirrel. While working at Angell Memorial Animal Hospital in Boston, someone brought in a little squirrel lying in a box. It was nearly dead anyway from a broken back, and Rose picked it up and put it to sleep. "Twenty minutes later, someone else comes in with another little squirrel in a box. And they say, it's a little squirrel with a broken back, can you put it to sleep? I didn't even really look at it," she relates. "I reach in there, and it screeches and leaps up . . . and it's hanging off my index finger! It hurt so bad that I had this horrible wall of pain at first, and then it diminished and I was laughing hysterically." She smiles in remembering. "All the techs are saying, 'Slam it against the wall!' And softie me, I look down and see those little brown eyes, and I just can't do it! Finally the ICU nurse comes in and pries it off my finger."

In this business you can't be afraid. But Rose, who treats elephants and sharks and snakes as well as birds and hedgehogs, says you have to be "respectful." Often, she says, owners or zookeepers who work with large and dangerous animals tell her that the animal won't hurt her. "They tend to say it repetitively," Rose says. But she would rather rely on her own instincts than someone else's reassurances. After all, the animal may know the keeper well but not Rose. Furthermore, Rose may be performing procedures that are confusing and painful.

Recently, Rose worked on an elephant in a small zoo who had an eye problem. She partnered with Dr. Anthony Moore, the ophthalmology specialist. "We were going to do some potentially painful things to her eye, and it was the first time we had ever worked with this elephant. I did not know that elephant, and I did not know these keepers."

The elephant was trained to lie down, but she was not restrained or chained. Rose, a former gymnast, says in these cases she stands in such a way that she can leap back quickly if necessary. "If you forget yourself, and get caught sitting on your haunches, you can really get hurt."

Surprisingly, elephants kill more keepers each year than any other animal. And when they do, there is no doubt that they mean harm. It takes a long time to get to know and trust an individual elephant.

Rose says one of the keepers laughed and asked her if she was afraid, an unprofessional and naïve question. "I said, I'm not afraid, but she's an elephant and I am aware of what she can do."

Later, the senior keeper told her this particular elephant used to be "a striker," an elephant that hits with its trunk. Considering that their tiny tails can club a person like a baseball bat and that the trunk itself is as tall and heavy as a man, a striker is a very dangerous animal, indeed.

At least with elephants and other fellow mammals, it's

easier to read their intentions. But how about reptiles? One keeper Rose works with has raised an anaconda from the time it was a baby. He feels completely comfortable with the snake, which is now 180 pounds. Rose, on the other hand, likes to be cautious with him.

She developed a close working relationship with the New England Aquarium vet, and the first time she was scheduled to cover for him when he was away, the snake developed a skin condition and needed a biopsy. That meant Rose had to punch out a little area of skin to examine in the lab. The keeper was sitting in the small enclosure with the snake's head and upper body on his lap when Rose arrived. He told Rose to come on in and do the biopsy.

"I said, 'Scott, I can't do anything for you if she wraps around you.' And so I nicely had to say, 'You have to come out of the enclosure.' "

Being a fill-in vet is like being a substitute teacher. All hell always breaks loose on your watch. That very same day, Rose had an even bigger challenge at the aquarium: she had to collect blood from a tiger shark without giving up any of her own.

"The women divers went into the big tank and went after that tiger shark with a sling," Rose recalls. As incredible as it sounds, the divers acted like rubber-suited cowpokes at roundup time.

"So they cornered this big old shark. And he kept tearing out of the shelter—it looked like something out of *National Geographic* where the guys are in the shark cage and the mouth is coming at you. I thought he was just going to nail them!" Rose was positioned just above, watching the commotion and standing ready with a needle. Every time she hesitated at reaching down to this thrashing bucket of teeth, the divers would shout, "Keep trying! Keep trying!"

So Rose did. "Finally! With my last stick, I got the blood collection."

Rose says it's all part of the challenge of dealing with a wide variety of animals and their owners. "There are a lot of subtle interactions that enable you to keep your body intact." It's a fine art that all vets must learn.

OF ANOREXIC SNAKES, MYOPIC KANGAROOS, AND MITE-Y HEDGEHOGS

AS quiet and unassuming as she is, Dr. Rosemarie Borkowski is quite accustomed to being the center of attention. When her patients arrive, they frequently cause a stir in the waiting room, and when they are taken back for examination, they can draw a stampede of otherwise sedate staff members who come, like excitable kids, to stare and giggle.

Rose's clients have sought medical help for their zebras, kangaroos, elephants, emus, ostriches, whales (though these have not been taken to the waiting room), and, more often, snakes, parrots, African hedgehogs, and turtles.

Her practice includes surprising skills such as chinchilla dentistry. These cute, soft-furred rodents of South America with the bushy tails are not obsessed with a bright white smile; it's just that the foods they eat in captivity don't grind their teeth down the way their fibrous diet does in the wild. Then they drool, and they can't eat.

It's no easy task to work on them. "They have the smallest oral orifice in the world. I mean, it's just really, really hard to get into their mouths," Rose says, laughing in mock frustration.

"The problem they are usually having is with their molars in the back, so you have to knock them down [anesthetize them] and really open up their mouths so that you can get back there and clip them."

Besides curing drooling chinchillas, she sees patients like Kibo, an African grey parrot who needs a health certificate so she can fly to West Palm Beach for the winter—using a commercial airline, that is, not her own wings.

African greys—chunky-looking parrots with light faces, gray bodies, and bright red tail feathers—are so smart and talkative, they've been dubbed "flying primates."

Kibo, like many birds, is shy of strangers, but Rose manages to win her over. She trims her toenails, removes a leg band, and even gets a blood sample from the eight-month-old bird's jugular vein. The veterinarian talks with the owner about care and diet, and learns that Kibo gets low-fat seeds, fruits, vegetables, and one other staple—Cheez-Its. When the examination is over, Kibo is declared healthy, and she is cleared for departure.

The patients right after Kibo couldn't be more different. A clean-cut, soft-spoken man brings in two African pygmy hedgehogs, animals that have become popular in the pet trade. As he talks about Chizzy and Henrietta, it is clear that he and his wife dote on the animals. It also becomes clear that they are being fed the wrong diet (including high-fat, high-protein cat food) and that Henrietta has become dangerously obese. While the young Chizzy is as small as a Beanie Baby, Henrietta resembles a grapefruit rolled in thumbtacks. Furthermore, her skin is sore and cracked, leading Rose to suspect a bad case of mites—the minute bugs that can infest animals. No wonder she is so unhappy. She has rolled into a ball, which is the standard hedgehog defense, and puffed herself up, all the while hissing like an angry punctured bicycle tire.

Henrietta is so obese that it changes the appearance of her hind end, and Rose isn't even sure initially that she is a female. Placed into a small glassed-in chamber that can be filled with anesthetic gas, Henrietta is knocked out. She then is removed, limp, from the enclosure. Rose confirms that she is indeed female and that she is crawling with mites. She is also suffering from a raging case of ulcerative dermatitis, a skin disorder. It's time for the hedgehog spa treatment.

Unrolling rolls of fat to clean the skin folds, Rose discovers how smelly Henrietta is. Rose simply wrinkles her nose, chuckles, and goes back to cleaning the skin with a long cotton swab. She also cleans discharge and mites from Henrietta's ears. Rose will prescribe Ivermectin, as she says, "for all your parasite needs." By the time everything is done, Henrietta begins groggily to awaken from the anesthesia.

Henrietta, now dopey, but fresh as a daisy, is returned to her owner, who says protectively, "She's so sensitive." He coos at her and looks concerned at her sleepy state. Rose goes over the medication and care with him and tells him to switch Henrietta and Chizzy's diet from hedgehog and cat food to dog food, cottage cheese, and eggs, plus a variety of insects.

The attachments people form with exotic animals can be as strong as they are with more traditional pets. That's especially true of some of the big exotic birds who can live eighty years or more. The emotions Rose has are as intense as in any other part of the hospital.

"I still get really upset about having to euthanize animals. I've always been in situations where I have the care of animals from beginning to end. Sometimes, if you're a specialist, you may have only part of a case, and you're not responsible for every single thing that happens. But many vets, including exotics practitioners, deal with every medical event an individual pet has, getting to know the owners very closely as well. Breaking the news about an animal's irreversibly declining status and performing euthanasia are difficult tasks that never really get easier. It takes a toll on veterinarians, too."

The human factor can have poignant twists as well. Rose vividly remembers a recent case with a doctor. He called to have his rabbit come in right away, actually paging through to Rose. She thought it was a little weird, but figured he was getting special treatment because he was a physician.

"When I got into the exam room, the owner had brought in a young rabbit. The bunny had suddenly developed problems with his hind legs and could not walk very well at all. As the story unfolded, it became clear what the emergency was.

"The whole family was there, the father, the mother, and this beautiful little eleven-year-old girl. The reason why the father was so distraught was that his daughter had just been diagnosed that summer with multiple sclerosis. She was having leg weakness—the same symptoms the rabbit was having."

Rose examined the animal. "As it turned out," she says, "the rabbit had lymphoma. I pulled the mother aside to explain how severe the rabbit's illness was." The mother wanted desperately for there to be some hope for this beautiful young animal, but Rose knew she could offer them none.

"I told her we would have to put the rabbit down or allow it to die on its own. The mother just started crying," Rose recalls, "and I looked out of the corner of my eye at this lovely young girl with MS."

Along with small exotic pets, Rose has some higher-profile cases. These are patients who turn heads—like Quigley, the big, beautiful seven-year-old red kangaroo from a local petting zoo who has become nearly blind.

At nine o'clock in the morning on an unseasonably warm and bright December day, Quigley emerges from the back of a red and white truck that is specially outfitted with wood paneling on the inside walls and skylights on the roof.

Quigley from down under is as big as a person and covered in a soft coat that runs from brown to gray to cream.

The married couple who own the zoo—Larry Records and Alexandra Burpee—help the kangaroo jump down into the parking lot outside the large animal hospital.

Quigley, it seems, prefers women in general, and Alexandra in particular. She speaks softly to him, and he listens intently. Holding onto his haunches from behind to guide him into the building, Alexandra gently motions him through the doors and along the rubber-matted hallways to a large examining room in front of the rows of stalls. Quigley has a funny way of walking. He uses his small forelimbs, touching his paws, which look so much like hands, to the ground, and then delicately sliding his hind legs forward. Several times he stops, turns, and touches his nose to Alexandra's for reassurance.

Rose works with veterinary ophthalmology specialist Anthony Moore, who will perform the eye examination. The room is packed with students, interns, residents, and staffers. Quigley is a curiosity.

Dr. Moore enters and addresses Quigley. "Hi, sweetie."

"Oh," Alexandra warns, shaking her head, "he's going to turn into a monster."

Sure enough, just hearing that male voice, Quigley rises off his muscular haunches, using his tail to steady himself in tripod fashion to achieve his full height. At six feet tall, and bristling with aggression, he is menacing. Alexandra's husband, Larry, is a big man, in that John Wayne salt-of-the-earth style. Expertly, he grabs Quigley's long, thick, heavy tail to keep the kangaroo off balance. For the ophthalmologist to do his examination, it will take Larry, their regular veterinarian, Rob Nicholson, and Alexandra holding tight to keep Quigley still.

With the room lights extinguished, the ophthalmologist has a look into Quigley's milky gray right eye with his lighted opthalmoscope. Quigley doesn't like it and squirms against all the arms holding him. Anthony takes a reading with a pen-like instrument, touching it to both of Quigley's eyes. The left eye, which is enlarged, has glaucoma. He also has a cataract in his right.

Quigley is let loose as vets and owners discuss the problem.

Rose moves away from the crowd and approaches the animal, who wouldn't let other staffers come near him. She kneels on bended knee to look up at Quigley, who is docile now. The kangaroo begins to quietly investigate this large closed room.

Anthony Moore tells Larry and Alexandra that the eye with glaucoma should be *enucleated*, or removed. A prosthetic device can be inserted under the eyelid for cosmetic reasons, but he explains that it is one of the most painful eye surgeries. The specialist suggests instead that the eye be removed and the lid simply sutured shut over the empty socket. The right eye will require cataract surgery at some point, but it isn't immediately necessary.

As the discussion goes on, Quigley has crept toward the voice of his tormentor, the ophthalmologist, and once again the kangaroo rears up to full height, this time lashing out with those stunted-looking forelimbs. Larry and Rob pull him back again.

Quigley will need some medication in his right eye, since the eyelid does not close completely over the eye. As a result, it has been exposed to air and dust. Usually, blinking cleans and protects the vulnerable moist eye, but Quigley has been unable to do this properly.

It's upsetting news for Larry and Alexandra. They've had a rash of bad luck this fall, with several of their animals getting sick. Their compassion toward their animals is almost legendary among the staff here, but a zebra with a tumor, a toucan with liver disease, and a camel that broke his leg out in a field have left them financially strapped.

Sympathetic, Anthony Moore says that the cataract surgery will cost about $750, not including anesthesia. Add to that several hundred for the enucleation, and then even more for boarding a large animal. Anthony tells them that this sort of surgery for a dog runs about $1,400 to $1,500, so Quigley's price would probably be about $1,500 or $2,000. He and one of the residents try to think of ways to cut costs and get that figure down.

Larry asks how much sight will be restored and wonders if the animal isn't better off the way he is. Blind, Quigley has been very conservative in his movements. With just a little sight, Larry worries that the animal will become too confident, attempt more movement, and get himself injured. It's a dilemma for which the vet staff has no clear answer.

Again, Quigley seeks comfort from Alexandra. She is five-eight and the kangaroo easily adjusts his height to nuzzle his face to hers. After a moment she turns and looks at Larry. "I just don't know if we can do it."

The couple has a lot to think about with this animal who has absolutely no business value to them now, but a great deal of sentimental worth. "If you even come to Tufts," Larry says, "the bill automatically costs more than the animal." But then he tips his hand and reveals that he's different from others he knows in the world of exhibiting animals. "A lot of people have animals to make money. We get the money so we can have animals."

Rose's rapport with Quigley is remarkable. Making contact is one of the biggest challenges of the job and, when accomplished, among the most rewarding.

"One of the things I really enjoy the most about working with the library of species I do is that every different species, and then individuals within that species, has their own way. I mean, they really do have personalities. A lot of times it's a matter of going slowly enough with them or just trying to observe them and just trying to understand what their language is that gives you so much information regarding how to approach them. Do you have to grab them up in a towel, or can you slowly approach them? Should you talk to them? Should you not talk to them? Should you pet them? Should you not pet them?"

She goes on, "I really like the iguanas. You know, with some of them you stroke them over their forehead where their little pineal gland is. They just close their eyes and rest— then you can perform an ultrasound exam on them in which nobody's stressed out, nobody has to get drugs or tranquilizers. The art of handling individual animals is the part of my work I most enjoy."

The knack cannot be learned in a book. "That's the sort of intuitive and kinesthetic awareness that you develop by working with a lot of different species," she says. "Like how fast you go—it makes such a huge difference."

That difference can have serious consequences. Rabbits are one of the species that is the most difficult to work with. "They are so fragile and they get so scared," Rose says. "Handling them can be such an intensive experience. You're literally afraid they're going to drop dead on you." The animals can become so frightened that they can, indeed, drop dead in the office, especially if they're there for treatment of an underlying illness. Other vets have had panicked rabbits leap free, only to fall off the table and break their backs.

Rose has felt blessed to enter the worlds of some species— both physically and emotionally. Before becoming a vet, for instance, she worked as a dolphin trainer.

"When I was working with dolphins, I was in the water with them every single day." Rose came to know them as distinct individuals. "They were very, very different individually, and it wasn't like they were all brilliant, or all sweet, or all any one way. They could be nasty, they could be whatever. But I saw that same breadth of expression of emotion, and the desire to control one's environment—to make decisions during the day—that I see in our own species."

Because Rose had been a gymnast growing up, she recognized in these animals a joy of athletic freedom and physical precision and strength. "There was this dolphin named Dawn," she recalls. "I was sitting out back on the dock one day, and out of the blue, she threw this triple spiral forward flip!" It was not part of the show routine, or anything that she had been trained to do. "One of the other, older trainers told me that she'd always thrown that flip. She'd made it up herself." So the trainers decided to use Dawn's maneuver. "They put a hand signal to it, and now she could do it on command. But no other dolphin did that."

Because of her background, Rose was especially appreciative of the move. "I knew from being a gymnast that there's a moment before executing a stunt in which you have to imagine your physical signature through space—you have to *see* yourself doing it—and that's an artistic, imaginative event, to envision the maneuver before its precise execution."

It was, for Rose, an epiphany. "It was a leap of understanding that crystallized in that moment, that dolphins had a similar capacity to our own.

"When you spend hours of time with dolphins or with other species, you have full eye contact with them, and you look back and forth at one another countless times. When you can slow down long enough and actually have time to interact with your patients—those are the best moments. That's when expansion of one's own imagination occurs, when considering the way of animals actually informs us.

"They have a completely different form of expression, a different form of communication or intelligence or whatever we want to trip up on calling it. There is this other being there—and I love the interaction."

* * *

A few stalls down from this examining room, Larry Records and Alexandra Burpee have another animal waiting for care at Tufts—a zebra who is back for a second round of chemotherapy. Rose does not participate in this procedure, but she is available to the zoo couple as they try to sort out how they will proceed.

Tutone, or Tuey for short, is a Grant's zebra. He originally came to Tufts the month before. Just in front of his right eye, a nasty red tumor juts out from the zebra's black-and-white-striped face in shocking technicolor. It is a *sarcoid*, or cancerous growth, that has been determinedly returning no matter how often it is removed or, as the doctors say, "debulked."

The month before, when Larry first swung the trailer carrying Tuey into the Tufts parking lot, he had assumed the animal would require major surgery, a procedure that would remove the zebra's eye. But that November day was to be one of surprises.

Just getting the animal into the barn was an accomplishment. Zebras have never been domesticated. They are wild, powerful creatures with a kick that is legendary among those who know. The sound of one zebra kicking another is "enough to make your teeth ache," as a retired zookeeper once put it. And they can kick out with the front as well as the hind hooves.

"You can never expect them to be a horse," Larry says. "You can get a good friendship with a zebra. But it's not a kissy one like with a cat."

As Larry walks the zebra into the hospital, accompanied by Tuey's comfort companion, a llama named Orville, everyone gives them a wide berth. Many of the large-animal experts stare in disbelief at the sight of a zebra who is gentle enough to be led in by a halter.

Tufts happens to have two A. Moores on staff—one is Anthony, the ophthalmologist, and the other is Antony, an Australian who is a staff oncologist. Both Moores start off on this case. But after some consideration Tony Moore believes that removing the zebra's eye will be unnecessary. That takes the eye doctor Moore off the case.

Tony Moore believes that all previous attempts to get rid of this mass simply were not aggressive enough. The plan today will be to knock Tuey out, debulk the tumor, and then really hit it hard with chemotherapy. In this instance that means injecting the powerful drug Cisplatin directly into the site. Two more applications of the drug will be required down the road, and working on a zebra is not easy. Tony says, "Too bad he's not a poodle."

As the team discusses the tough task of getting a needle into this dangerous animal, a top-gun horse surgeon, Dr. Carl Kirker-Head, walks by. Smirking, he says, "And don't forget, we want a rectal temp taken on him too." Everyone laughs, and at that moment Tuey, whose halter is being pulled, bares his teeth, sets his ears back, and jerks his head. "We have racehorses who behave worse than that," the horse surgeon says.

Resident Dr. Jose Garcia is the hit man. He is able to stick a sturdy needle in quickly and plunge a syringe full of sedative into Tuey's thigh as Larry holds the halter tight against the bars of the stall. Preparation is made for the anesthesia catheter, a difficult procedure because the skin of zebras is so much thicker and tougher than that of horses. The flexible tubing that is inserted into the vein often collapses under the pressure of the thick skin.

While waiting for Tuey to go down, a sign is placed outside his stall: NO CROWDS, PLEASE. CAUTION: DO NOT ENTER STALL. PLEASE GIVE ZEBRA HIS SPACE.

The mood lightens as Tuey's lids begin to droop. Larry looks around at the group of staffers and says wryly, "By the way, in my opinion, they're white with black stripes."

By two-thirty it seems safe enough for a vet tech to enter the stall and insert a neck catheter. It is through this device that the anesthesia and other drugs will be administered.

Larry warns her, "Careful, when the lights come on with him, they come on fast."

Once the catheter is in place, Tuey, drowsy but still capable of walking, is led down to a pre-op room. Because this surgery does not have to be sterile (the cutting will not be deep), the entire procedure will take place here.

Only a few team members enter the small, padded room with Larry. Behind the closed door, they are able to quiet the animal in order to start anesthesia. Once that is flowing, Tuey slumps to the floor, which is covered with a thick vinyl-covered cushion. The animal that is often described as "a horse in pajamas" is now sound asleep.

Once the tumor, which looks like a double strawberry rolled in dirt, is scrubbed clean, it is a bright, angry red. Jose, kneeling on the blue cushion, takes a scalpel and slices right through the base of it.

Standing in the position directly behind the zebra's hind end, veterinarian Rob Nicholson suddenly waves the air around him and makes a face at an odor. "Oh, sure," a technician deadpans, "blame the zebra." Everyone has a good laugh.

Once Jose has removed the entire mass, oncologist Tony Moore arrives. He's sporting dark blue heavy latex gloves. As Jose and an assistant cauterize the site to stop the bleeding, Tony prepares the syringe with the highly toxic cream-color medicine. He injects a little at a time all around and in the area of the tumor, saturating the site with chemicals to kill off the cancer cells.

Once this cutting-edge medical procedure is finished, the veterinarians take advantage of the zebra's slumber and clean his teeth with an instrument that looks like a huge screwdriver.

By five o'clock, Tuey is up and ready to kick down the stall walls. The team sends him home and hopes for the best.

Tuey will come in for two more treatments of Cisplatin,

and months later there will still be no sign of recurrence. Jose reports that even the stripes grew back in correctly.

It is an odd, if exciting, world that Rose Borkowsi travels in. What could have led her here?

Rose always thought about being a veterinarian—her three loves were "athletics, music, and animals." But not until after college did she begin to focus on the prospect.

"When I got done with college, I was actually teaching high school science. I was biking a lot, and I kept coming across hurt birds. Back when I was a kid, I had always taken care of hurt birds. My family did little mini wildlife rehab when I was a young girl. I did a lot of ducks since we lived on a lake. I love birds and had always wanted to fix them up and let them fly away."

That's when she saw an ad for dolphin trainers. She jokes that the small aquarium had such high turnover that "they were grabbing women off the streets and putting them in bathing suits."

They paid only $4.50 an hour, but the experience proved to be critical. "That's when some of the experiences that I had had crystallized, and I decided that I really did want to go to school. I wanted to be in a position to help these animals.

"I always had in my mind the picture of a veterinarian being a person who could take care of any animal. But it was a surprise to go to veterinary school and just pretty much get dog and cat stuff. And some horses, but that was it. We really didn't learn that much about birds at all. A lecture here, a lecture there, but very little hands-on stuff and no wildlife."

That didn't sit well with Rose. From the experiences she'd had as a child growing up in the outdoors in South Florida, plus all the time as a dolphin trainer, she wanted to be able to treat all different kinds of species.

The opportunity came after she had started private practice. "That's when I read there was a position at the Wildlife

Clinic open for a one-year internship. And so I went up here and did another $15,000-dollar-a-year internship." She learned about birds, and she also found herself falling in with people at the New England Aquarium. So at the same time she learned more about aquatic wildlife, too.

That led to meeting some of the world's leading scientists, and Rose herself was able to raise some grant money to do research on harbor porpoises. Her career has gone on some exotic tangents, but all she has wanted is simply to "be able to treat whatever species comes in the door."

She is in the right place. Some strange animals do come through the doors at Tufts. Like an anorexic anaconda who needs an endoscopy.

The New England Aquarium came to Rose in desperation. Their prize three-and-a-half-year-old green anaconda had not eaten in five months. Though these snakes normally go a few months without food, five is dangerous. Anacondas are the largest snakes in the world, and there have been rare documented cases of their killing and swallowing humans. The patient this day, however, is only twelve pounds. Still, he does have sharp teeth set into his gums, so caution is required.

The plan is to "snake" an endoscope, a long, flexible tube, through the mouth, into its digestive tract. Using bright light and fiber optics, it will provide a detailed view to doctors on a television screen.

Crowded into the tiny endoscopy room are Rose; Dr. Orla Mahony, an endoscopy expert; a veterinarian and a handler from the aquarium; a technician to handle the anesthesia; and curious students, techs, and other vets.

Scott, the snake's handler, brings the patient out of its travel case. It is an army green color with brown spots, many of them with a splash of yellow.

Rose uses an instrument that looks like a little wedged spatula to prop open the snake's mouth. She eases an anesthetic tube into the snake's trachea. In the wild, this snake would use its numerous sharp teeth to grab prey and then coil his body around to suffocate the victim. Rose, in green jeans and a white lab coat over a striped blue wool sweater, puts her fingers right into the snake's mouth. "Let me know when his tail starts to go limp," she says to Andrea Osborne, the aquarium vet, who is posted at the other end of the snake.

Soon it is limp enough to begin. Orla measures the endoscope's tubing along the length of the snake's body to be sure it is long enough, then begins the procedure. First the room is darkened. On the TV screen, mounted high up on the wall, the fantastic journey begins with a clear view of the wet, pink gums inside the mouth. A bubbly underwater sound from the equipment adds to the atmosphere. Taking the tube out again for a second, the device suddenly shows a slightly out-of-focus view of the room, and everyone in it, before the scope is reinserted and the crowd gets to spelunk down the snake's throat.

Orla, who has inserted endoscopes in all kinds of cats and dogs, is amazed at "how vascular" the snake's esophagus is—the pink tunnel is mapped with countless spidery veins.

This is truly uncharted territory: No one in the room has ever seen inside a snake before. No one has ever seen photos of it before. The entire process is one of discovery—for the experienced snake handlers and endoscope doctor alike.

As the light passes down its route, it shines through the snake's body—a warm red circle ever so slowly drifting down from mouth to tail. Up on the screen, the view passes through what seems to be miles of pink, wet digestive tract—the highway of no return for many animals.

At times, portions of the tract appear to come to dead ends. But with a little push of the endoscope, these blind ends open up, revealing themselves to be sphincters, muscular doorways that shut tight between segments of digestive tract. In coming to the second sphincter, no one is sure if that means they have already passed through the stomach.

"There are hundreds of different kinds of snakes," Rose explains, "and there is great variation among them. Some have a little teeny left lung; some of them have a long left lung. There's a lot of variation in the way that they metabolize drugs. And I *might* find one or two articles on doing endoscopy in snakes, but I haven't found anything on endoscopy in anacondas." So there are many unknowns. What they are looking for are signs of cryptosporidium [a parasite], tumors, or infectious problems.

As they enter what they believe to be the small intestine, the aquarium's vet, who has been monitoring the snake's vital signs, warns that he is "getting tone back," meaning muscle tone, meaning he could be waking up. The anesthesia is increased slightly.

By now the red light is far down the length of the snake. In fact, the entire one-meter length of the scope has disappeared inside it. Rose announces that she will mark lengths as the endoscope is slowly being retracted so that they can map out everything they have seen. Yet before that starts, at the scope's farthest point, suddenly they make a discovery.

Large red blotchy lesions mark the walls. The lesions have striations running up them, giving them the texture of corrugated metal. It's time for a mucosal biopsy. A tool is inserted through the endoscope that will snip tiny tissue samples for collection. Working these clippers, which Rose triggers at several of the plaque-like sites, is tedious work, and each sample must be placed on a slide and marked with its location.

Orla, who speaks with a charming brogue, often begins her remarks by saying, "You know, Rose." Now she says, "You know, Rose, I'm not sure where a large bowel would start in a snake."

As they puzzle over the position of the sphincters, Rose says, "They're so carnivorous, I wonder if they just have small stomachs." Herbivores need larger guts to process plant material with its tough cell walls.

Then Orla wonders aloud about the evolution of the snake. "Why is their esophagus so long? What's the point of that?"

Andrea injects two syringes of electrolyte solution into the snake to ensure he does not become dehydrated during the process. The injections, just under the skin, leave two ping-pong ball–size lumps on the snake's body.

Captive snakes can have liver problems from a fatty diet, and the team thinks the striations could point to that. They decide that as long as the snake is still drowsy, they'll try running him over to ultrasound for a quick look at his liver.

Eventually, when all the medical evidence is considered, Rose says that the anaconda is actually quite well. Even the red striations turn out to be perfectly normal tissue. A clean bill of health, however, does not inspire the anaconda to start eating, so the aquarium decides to send him to a snake "shrink." An expert in behavioral modification for snakes will work to adjust the anaconda's environment and prey menu to see what makes it feel comfortable enough to eat.

Understanding animals is at the core of treatment. "I remember an old sea lion that they had at the New England Aquarium. Dr. Krum, Dr. Moore, and I were doing eye exams on him. He's twenty-three or twenty-four years old. Big male sea lion. Huge—six hundred or seven hundred pounds. And he was exquisitely trained. I mean, he had such a sense of trust. He would just look at his trainers and do everything that they wanted him to do, but he had a little wariness because we were doing some things that hadn't been done before."

Muggy would keep looking back at his trainers and then at the doctors until "this moment when he like really looked at me," Rose says. "You have that moment, you know you're not expecting it, you're not looking for it to happen, but you have a sudden understanding that the animal has a huge amount of awareness. And it makes you wonder."

This brings to mind a book she once read. A European came to the United States and interviewed an old, nearly illiterate Lakota Indian named Lame Deer, who had become very wise in his old age. "He came to have a sense of understanding of history and his own place in the world that was so profound." There is one thing he said, above all else, that Rose feels guides her in her thinking about animals: "Man is in great need of mystery—he cannot live without it."

For Rose, this concept is so simple and yet so profound. "Sometimes in science and in medicine, there's this constant desire to know things immediately. It's part of our biological heritage to figure things out. But sometimes," she points out, "our pride or ego gets so involved that we are afraid to step back a little bit and let the answer come to us."

Rose says she thinks of the European and the Indian, separated by language but able to communicate nonetheless. Their relationship was like Rose's with a dolphin, "and other animals who don't speak English very well," she says. "So that's a metaphor that I will always remember."

Rose finds herself evaluating her work on a philosophical level. "There are different phases of our lives that we go through," she says. At this point she's tired of the overemphasis on science and technology as applied to medicine. "It's always, 'What do you know?' 'What can you do?' We're constantly trying to manipulate things. And we're so afraid to wait a few days or a couple of weeks to really watch an animal and fully understand its response to a disease or to medical therapy.

"In a setting like this where there are lots of cases, and lots of people, the individual doctors aren't with the animals for very long each day. Sometimes we rely too much on lab work, radiographs, or other scientific tests to make care management decisions, and not enough on simple observations of individual animals."

Rose recalls a case from the time she was in vet school. From her own observations, she believed a horse with a massive infection was getting better, though the lab tests were not showing improvement. This was because, like many students, she walked the animals at night. "You could really get a sense of how they were doing because you were with them so much. This young horse had a horrible salmonella infection, and then she went into renal failure, and her kidney value was off the wall. She was hospitalized for weeks. On paper, it looked like she was getting worse, but she was actually getting better. She especially liked to go for walks in the moonlight, when it was cool. And she would whinny if you brought her fresh grass.

"The doctors were convinced they had to put her to sleep because her creatinine, or kidney value, was so high. It was difficult to convey to them that she was actually improving, because during the day they just got a quick glimpse of her standing forlornly in a dark, dank isolation stall. She was really a different horse when she went outside, but they never saw that."

One day euthanasia was scheduled for one o'clock. The owner had spent thousands on the horse and deeply cared for her. As a student, it was not Rose's place to make her views known. But she did. She told the owner she felt that the horse was getting better despite what the lab results said.

The horse made it home and even became a show animal. Rose remembers the story as a reminder to consider more than lab results when deciding the fate of an animal.

Her intuition continued to develop. Rose remembers a case that turned out to be one of the most important lessons of her life. A baby barred owl was brought in with a bad laceration on her head. It was full of maggots. By the time Rose saw it, the case had been sitting at the clinic for more than a day. The little bird couldn't hold its head up.

The hospital had a lot of cases that day, and she didn't have another doctor on with her. Other experienced techs were telling her that the animal was full of maggots, which probably had all kinds of toxins, and she should just put it to sleep. "But I kept thinking, I should at least sedate the bird and find out how bad the wound is. See if there was any chance that she could live."

The clinic was so busy all day that the case of the little owl had to wait. All the while, Rose was working nonstop. By evening, she was exhausted. Plus, so many hopeless cases come into wildlife rehabilitation clinics in the spring that euthanasias are countless. "At that particular time of the year, you're doing cases six or seven days a week," Rose says. "You go over the case. You put it down. It takes a toll on you. And you get so exhausted in having to make decisions to put things to sleep. I put down more animals in that one year than a lot of vets put down in several."

The last thing Rose wanted to do at the end of this punishing day was to put the baby owl to sleep. But she also didn't have the energy to treat her properly. "I thought, I can't get to her today. I'm just going to have to put her to sleep. So I pulled up the blue juice, and I had her restrained. I was just about to inject her with it, but she was really struggling." She remembers feeling, "This animal still has a lot of life in her."

Rose hesitated with the tiny bird struggling in her hands. Rose was struggling too. Just then a colleague came by and said that if the little owl made it, there would likely be a place for her to live in captivity, if she could not be returned to the wild.

Rose stopped what she was doing. She didn't kill the bird, and she didn't begin surgery in her exhausted, useless state. Instead, she put the little bird back in the cage and went home to bed.

"The next day we came in—I started fresh and we anesthetized her. I pulled out loads of maggots from her head." All the while the other techs kept saying she was probably going to die, "but she still had all this life in her. We pulled the maggots out of her, and she could lift her head up. And she did great."

The little bird, remarkably, was adopted by another bird in the wildlife center—Archie, a captive barred owl who is female. Archie, who has only one wing and cannot be released, was the center's mascot.

"Archie would feed that baby. We got all kinds of really great publicity for it. Plus it taught a lot of wildlife rehabbers that a female owl that's never had babies before will potentially take a foster baby. That's not well documented. We have great pictures of them munching on mice together."

The baby owl grew big and strong enough to live out its life, as it should, in the wild. "A little high school girl got to be involved in letting her go," Rose says, "and it was the greatest thing that happened to this little girl in her life."

Maybe that's how wildlife vets are hatched.

ON A WING
AND A PRAYER

EVEN blindfolded and spun around, you would know if you were led into the Wildlife Clinic at Tufts University School of Veterinary Medicine. Though the crooked and bent little white house that serves as the clinic is kept spotlessly clean, there is a gamy, musty aroma that unmistakably says "wildlife."

Here, on a far corner of the campus, a steady stream of patients—1,200 to 1,500 a year—arrives in shoeboxes, blankets, and towels. Injured mice, chipmunks, turtles, owls, red-tailed hawks, sharp-shinned hawks, swans, peregrine falcons, woodpeckers, mink, deer, porcupines, and cormorants receive medical care here. They've been hit by cars, shot, or tangled in wires. Sometimes they have odd problems, like the wild turkey who was "egg bound," or unable to lay eggs that were ready to come out. That has to be uncomfortable.

The problems are seasonal, according to the head of the clinic, Dr. Mark Pokras. There's baby season (April through summer); hunting season (fall); botulism season, when animals are feeding off of spoiled trash or carcasses (summer); and starving or dehydration season (winter).

These animals can be dangerous or diseased, and yet "the public brings them in," Mark Pokras says, "either because they're brave or naïve." But above all, he says, they are caring.

There's always a story. One cormorant, too sick to fly, was found walking down the middle of the street in a suburban neighborhood. Two cats trailed him menacingly. He turned out to be "tough as nails," according to one staffer, and he recovered nicely from the puncture wounds that were discovered and treated.

A tiny deer mouse arrives one day in a photo box lined with bed linens. The young hairdressing salon owner who brings it in says her cat injured the little animal. The woman is distraught, not because the cat had placed the injured mouse on her pillow while she was sleeping, but because she's worried about the little creature. It's so cute and helpless.

She says she tried giving it—what else?—cheese, but it wouldn't eat. Dr. Elizabeth Stone explains that the mouse might be beyond help, but that she will do what she can. She determines that the little brown mouse with the fluffy white belly and mangled back leg is too ill to save. A syringe full of pink euthanizing solution puts it out of its misery. Case number 1,281 is recorded as "compromised mouse."

The mouse is one of the species that might be thought too common to bother with. With all the mice in the world, why spend the time and money? Yet even individuals from very common species—pigeons, squirrels, crows, and Canada geese—receive care.

Part of the reason is that the students need to learn on something, and better that they learn on a species not in jeopardy than an endangered one. But the issue of who is worth saving and who isn't is a complicated matter. Mark says one of the most important aspects of the students' training is that a thoughtful, unhurried discussion takes place each time to hash out those intense philosophical questions.

He points out that some rehabilitators will not take non-native animals, or game animals, or animals that are too common. It's a question of allotting resources. The students who spend time at the clinic have to make those decisions often.

"The students have to make their own decisions, but they have to understand the breadth of decision-making here. These are difficult issues, and we don't have easy answers. What is the appropriate role for humans in the grand scheme of things? It's not just the welfare of the individual animal," Mark says. "Introduction of exotic species, habitat destruction, human population issues—you get into some very fundamental philosophical, ecological, economic, social issues."

What Mark believes personally about all this "differs on different days, to be honest," he says. Because his job entails playing God in the clinic, Mark says for him, an important element is to always examine his motives.

Not surprisingly, he confesses, "I like some animals better than others. Some just tug at my heartstrings." That makes sense, but his choices are probably not those that most people would pick. He is not drawn to the bunnies and fawns. "Aquatic birds, waterfowl, cormorants, and gulls," he says, listing his favorites. These birds are usually the most pungent, and the most aggressive in fending off treatment. But Mark finds them "endearing, responsive, and behaviorally complex." Birds of prey, he says are "sexy and neat," but not as bright as aquatic birds. With raptors, "it's all vision," he says.

Even animals one might consider positively unsightly—the opossum, for example—attract this wildlife veterinarian. What many of us see in this species is a rat-like face and tail, and a round torso covered in mangy fur. That's not what Mark sees.

He becomes almost rhapsodic in describing a "big old male opossum" currently being treated. The animal was hit by a car and sustained "ten or twelve skull fractures" as well as a broken tooth. Though he came in at death's door, he received fluids and TLC, and even had that troublesome tooth pulled by a veterinary dentist. What Mark admires is this animal's—and the species'—awesome ability to endure.

"Opossums are remarkable survivors. They're very endearing. What I see is an amazing animal—North America's only marsupial. An animal with a tremendously long genealogy. Something that has out-competed most of the placental mammals since before the last Ice Age. And it's extending its range"—it has traveled north, coming to New England in the last several decades, and now it has reached Canada. Opossums are the ultimate omnivores. If there's anything out there, they'll eat it, and survive on it, and reproduce on it, and do well. And I find that amazing—surviving and thriving in spite of all the terrible things humans do to the planet."

Regardless of personal wildlife preferences, resources have to be managed. The clinic cannot make an all-out effort to save every creature who is brought in; there simply isn't enough money. Yet even if these animals are not beloved pets, their lives do count. And the methods of treating them are passed on to the scores of students studying wildlife medicine.

All sorts of interesting tricks of the trade prove vital to saving these creatures. Cormorants, who are diving birds, do not have nostrils. That's important to know because if one were to try to tape the beak shut in order to work on it, the animal would not be able to breathe. When cornered, these birds aim their sharp beaks right for your eyes, so staffers have to wear safety goggles—another important item to consider.

Often, birds will peck at anything white, so gauze bandages placed on them are usually covered over with a dark stretchy tape.

Whereas mammals are shaved in preparation for surgery, birds are prepared in a different fashion. A "plucking bowl" is provided in the operating room to toss the feathers cleared from the surgical site.

These are the kinds of procedures that three fourth-year

vet students learn during their two-week rotation here. In the basement of the building, where the patients are housed in cages, Dr. Elizabeth Stone is giving the three students—Mary Masterson, E. Sunshine Eckstrom, and Alison Hayward—pointers on how to get a red-tailed hawk out of a cage.

"Don't be afraid," Elizabeth says, "he won't hurt you. When you go to grab him, he'll go up. So anticipate that." She recommends a fast, determined capture. "You can't hurt him out here, even when he's flapping around," she says, "but you could in there if you futz around."

Alison is the first to try. She opens the door of a large wooden enclosure that stands at chest height. With a hand protected by a large leather glove, she makes a grab, and a cloud of tiny downy feathers shoots out as in some comedy film with a pillow fight.

After a second attempt, her gloved hand emerges with a flailing hawk on it. He hangs upside down, flapping his great wings wildly. Then he flips up, sitting tall on the glove.

"Keep his feet away from your stomach," Elizabeth says, "and keep his face away from your chest. He's not bitey, but they can grab a nipple." Everyone winces and laughs.

In general, birds of prey are docile and compliant once they are hooded and sitting on a glove. It's easy to see how falconers are able to take advantage of this when they start to train their birds.

The four women bring this majestic creature up to one of the surgery rooms on the first floor. The bones of his right wing have been broken, and he has already been operated on to place pins in his wing. Today he will be anesthetized so he can receive physical therapy—his wing will be manipulated and stretched ever so gently.

The students place him down on a thick pink towel laid out on a stainless steel examining table. Lying on his back, the bird's cream-colored chest and belly, flecked with chocolate-colored markings, are exposed.

A rubber bell is fitted over his beak and the anesthesia is pumped in. The bird's breathing becomes shallow, and his body goes limp.

A call comes through for Elizabeth, and while she is talking with a friend, the anesthetic in the vaporizer runs empty. No one is wearing the thick protective glove when the big bird with the huge beak and sharp claws awakens in a flash of panic.

Calmly, Elizabeth says into the phone, "Can you hold on a sec?"

As everyone else stares wide-eyed, she deftly pours more fluid into a vaporizer, watches the bird slump again, and then placidly resumes her conversation.

The students share meaningful glances, looking at each other in amazement, and then they unsuccessfully try to stifle a laugh. One of the most important lessons of the day is: Always stay calm.

The hawk is worked on, examined, and then rebandaged. Once he comes to, and before he's brought down to his cage, he is fed a dead mouse whose corpse has been spiked with antibiotics. As he perches on Alison's gloved hand, he gets a second mouse as a chaser.

Then he rejoins the other patients, who include a sick goose whose eyes are covered in white mucus; an adorable red screech owl who was hit by a car; and a Canada goose whose broken wing cannot be repaired.

Though there are some quiet afternoons, mornings at the clinic are always bustling as the patients are fed, cleaned, and medicated. Only days into their rotation, the students seem like old pros.

Each animal has different needs. Mary explains that the eastern box turtle will not eat or go to the bathroom before she's had a good soak. So she turns on the tap in a large sink, filling the area with tepid water. Within minutes there are results. Poop floats next to the turtle.

Turtle expert and veterinarian Barbara Bonner has already lectured these students on "the Zen of turtles," giving them a number of wonderful pointers. First and foremost, "a turtle deserves the same dignity that someone's prize poodle gets." She points out that turtles do everything slowly—including heal. "The reptile way of life is to conserve your energy, pull inside, and go on with life." Ultimately, she says with conviction, "Everybody can learn something from turtles."

On the kitchen counter is a box with recipes you would never find in Julia Child's kitchen.

BABY BIRD FORMULA

1 cup canned dog food (Ken-L Ration)
1/2 cup hi-protein (or mixed) baby cereal
2 hard-boiled egg yolks
6 tablespoons applesauce
1/4 teaspoon liquid multi-vitamins
1 50 mg calcium carbonate or gluconate tablet

Add water to mixture if it's too stiff. Put 2–3 tablespoons in a Ziploc bag.
Mush it down and freeze it, breaking pieces as needed.

Breakfast time at the clinic is enough to make you lose your own. The gulls get a mixture of dog food and fish. Mice are fed to the screech owl. The box turtle, glistening from her morning ablutions, ever so slowly downs her breakfast of baby mice (or in the lingo, "pinkies") and mouse parts.

With all the bathing and feeding, and airing outdoors, the clinic can sometimes seem like a wildlife spa, but very important healing work goes on here. Many of the animals are resilient and after treatment are returned to the wild. Some who have wings amputated, or have lost their sight, are turned over to rehabilitators or educators who will care for them in captivity.

Even so, the money isn't endless, and extreme measures cannot be taken to save every animal who comes through the doors. That would take up all the funds quickly and leave none for other animals who can be successfully treated. So those philosophical discussions Mark says are so important take place continually. Many animals inspire great discussion among the staffers—how far should we go? Does this one stand a chance?

One of those cases was a chubby young porcupine. It had been found in the woods in the western part of the state, lying out in the open, too sick to run away as a compassionate person approached.

The soft-looking chocolate-colored creature was laid out flat on its belly, a towel placed underneath him on an examining table in the clinic. He remained motionless—not a good sign at all. He was in shock, Elizabeth reported, meaning that from trauma, or blood loss, or infection, his circulatory system was going haywire. On examination it was clear that a back leg had been shattered, probably by a car.

Since he was a mammal and so ill, he might have rabies, too. Although anyone handling wildlife here has been inoculated against the virus, no one takes any chances. Everyone wears latex gloves. Vaccines are known to fail sometimes. "If anyone gets pricked by a quill," Elizabeth announces, "it should count as an exposure."

They place a heating pad under him and inject some fluids. A tube of soft brown paste is syringed into his mouth, and he swallows some of the mixture, which is high in sugar and vitamins. Then his snout is placed in a bell that delivers oxygen.

The porcupine looks like a cuddly stuffed toy, with two white buck teeth sticking out in front of his mouth and slender yellow quills speckling his soft brown fur. Even the pads on his feet, visible as he lies unconscious, look like the no-skid pads on a child's pajamas.

But cute or not, this small creature is in terrible shape. His temperature, which should be around 100 degrees, is only 90.1. Another heating pad is placed over him, and a hot water bottle is positioned between his back legs. A heating lamp is plugged in above him. A neck catheter is inserted, and he begins to receive a steady infusion of fluids.

His breathing starts to improve, and his pulse seems stronger. A student has trouble finding a vein to get a blood sample and says without irony, "It's hard to stick a porcupine."

His temperature is taken again, and it's come up to 96. Elizabeth, notes, though, that anything under all those heating pads would get hot—this rise in temperature is probably passive. He is most likely not stabilizing himself. More blood tests show that they've raised his blood-glucose level up to normal.

The little porcupine is still not responsive. "We've corrected everything we can correct," Elizabeth says, "but he's still out of it."

Since there is no porcupine blood available for transfusion, Elizabeth is beginning to think it's time to give up. Another vet happens by and agrees there are no other measures to be taken, except sending him "good karma," he says. Sunshine hears the comment and notes that his karma should be good on its own. "He's a porcupine. He's never done anything wrong."

By two o'clock, the young animal is clearly not getting better, and the pink euthanasia solution is injected into his neck catheter. It is an unhappy moment for everyone.

Rose Borkowski has spent time working in the Wildlife Clinic, and she knows only too well the feeling of defeat when putting one of these animals to sleep. She recalls a case that really got to her. It was a bald eagle who flew into some power lines while tussling with another eagle. The animal was electrocuted and fell to the ground, sustaining neurological damage.

"It lived through the burns, but it had gotten abnormalities of the spinal cord because of it," Rose says. "I worked with him for about six months." She knew there were several points at which she could legitimately have given up on the creature, but she felt the tug of a moral dilemma. The bird had flown into a power line, another victim of human society. "We do all these different things that cause wildlife to die."

Wild animals get hit by cars, electrocuted from power lines, and poisoned by manufactured products like antifreeze. They come to the clinic with bullet wounds and arrow punctures. Rose felt the need to fix at least one wrong civilization had committed against wild animals.

"I felt as responsible for that animal's death as anybody else," Rose says. "I could have been on the phone calling a wildlife organization trying to raise money for wildlife when it happened.

"I worked with that animal for six months and went through agonizing decisions several times about whether or not I had to put it to sleep. I kept going with the case," she recalls, "even when it looked hopeless. Ultimately, I had to put the bird down. That was a tough one."

After all that effort, she then felt a pang of guilt for trying so hard. "That's the other thing," she says, laughing a bit at herself. "All the energy that got put into that case maybe should have been put instead into others."

Fortunately, she has had many cases that have recovered, instances in which she felt that she had given a little bit back to nature. Ultimately, Rose says, no matter the outcome, working with wildlife is "a humbling experience."

Deciding which animals take priority is the daily struggle that colors all the activity here. "You're always second-guessing yourself. For every one like that little owl that made it, there are dozens and dozens and dozens in which you've put as much energy and they don't," Mark says. "You kick yourself around the block, saying I made that animal suffer for hours or even days because my ego was caught up in it.

"You keep wanting to do each case better. Doing the same as yesterday isn't good enough. You want to have learned something from your failures as well as your successes. Which ones should I have euthanized earlier? Which ones didn't I go far enough on? Which ones do we desperately need a new technique to approach?"

At the end of his career, Mark would like to be able to say, "I left things better than I found them, and I had fun." He tells all the vet students, "It's no use going through all the training unless you've had fun." He also appreciates the ripple effect of being an educator. "With my own actions I can change the world only so much. But if I can go out and interact with students, I can be evangelical and the circles get wider and wider and wider."

The doctrine he teaches has true power. All the science leads to a sense of accomplishment that is rather spiritual. Mark says it comes down to "a sense of being part of something much larger than oneself."

To release an injured bird who has been healed, Mark says, is "an amazing high." As you stand and watch such a creature take wing to freedom, "a part of you goes with it."

Even though that moment of release is absolute poetry in motion, Mark says true success is often measured much later. "I remember one time a great horned owl had been shot with a BB gun and lost one eye," he recalls. "I talked to a lot of people about it, and they assured me that if we released that bird, it wouldn't have much of any chance of surviving in the wild."

He did release the bird, anyway, and gave her a shot at a

natural life. But the real test of success in nature is reproduction, of course. "Two years later," Mark says proudly, "when we found her incubating eggs in the nest, that was really something. It was even better two years later."

WHY GORDON SETTERS AND PANTY HOSE DON'T MIX

DIETARY indiscretion is a clinical term, believe it or not, that describes the propensity of some pets to eat things that can be dangerous and even deadly. Cats are famous for ingesting "linear foreign bodies." They love to play with string. If they try to swallow it, though, one part can become wrapped around the base of the tongue, and then the rest of the length of string travels down to the stomach or even intestines. The string gets tangled and can cut through tissue as the gastrointestinal tract conducts its regular conveyor-belt movement called peristalsis. Dr. John Berg says, "the intestine literally crawls up the string." Any attempt by an owner to yank the string can make the condition worse. It's a job for a surgeon.

Dogs are generally not as picky as cats, and they get into a wider variety of these problems of indiscretion. They swallow all kinds of objects that won't pass through their systems. They also eat things that can make them terribly sick. Mushrooms in the yard, moldy food in the trash, rotting leaves, socks, and even sticks can make your pet ill.

Surgical resident Carolyn Garzotto has seen dogs' stomachs

"filled with rocks" along with pennies and toys. Because of a bet, John Berg's team actually counted the rocks, many just pebbles, that they pulled out of one dog's stomach—there were about two thousand.

In one famous case at Tufts, a dog ate some children's toys, and on X ray their shapes—a scorpion, a lizard, and a soldier—could clearly be seen.

Another instance was hardly a family matter. A physician came to the front desk one day and announced his dog had attempted to swallow a "marital device." It was now lodged in the dog's throat. In this case, too, X rays graphically depicted the outline of the object.

Of all the odd things he's removed from dog bellies, though, John says he's never taken out chicken bones—the one item so many of us worry about our dogs ingesting.

Dogs eat many funny things, but they are particularly drawn to items that smell just like their beloved owners. Dog trainer Brian Kilcommons likens this behavior—dogs chewing our personal things—to the way we sometimes fondly stroke a favorite photo of a loved one. Among the most common foreign bodies that surgeons remove from dogs' stomachs and intestines are socks, underwear, and panty hose.

That's precisely what got Kenzie, a lovable Gordon setter, into trouble.

Owner Chester Lay reported that Kenzie seemed particularly drawn to the undergarments of the females in the household. One fine fall day Kenzie binged on underpants and panty hose. (One surgeon at Tufts reports that on another case, the suspicious wife of an owner demanded to know the brand of panty hose recovered from the dog's gut.) All that bulky material jammed up Kenzie's system and made the dog very sick. He was rushed to a local vet, who performed surgery to remove the underthings within him, cutting into the intestine and colon to pull the twisted material out.

After surgery, though, Kenzie was sicker. Late in the day he was rushed to the emergency room at Tufts. Dr. Jana Norris, a surgical resident, was about to go off duty. But with the sick setter's arrival, she stayed.

Kenzie lay flat on his side. "Pus was just pouring out of the incision," she says. It was as foul as rotten cheese. The poor dog couldn't get up, but he would respond to his name, endearing himself to those admitting him.

Kenzie was so compromised that he could die under anesthesia or at any time during the first thirty-six hours after surgery.

Jana told Chester that Kenzie had only a 40 percent chance of surviving. Chester recalls the moment vividly. "I love that dog," he says, and he felt devastated by the news. This big eight-year-old setter was his hunting partner, going after pheasant and quail. He was a fit and enthusiastic gun dog.

Jana scrubbed up to do battle. She undid two feet of suturing on Kenzie's belly. When she opened up Kenzie's abdomen, she found that the far end of the colon, six to eight inches from the rectum, had been cut into. This is done only in extreme circumstances, when there is no choice but to operate on it. The colon is notorious for not healing very well, and many vets just hope that if a foreign object is way down there, it's on its way out on its own.

To make Kenzie's situation even worse, all the sites of the stomach, intestine, and colon that had been stitched were breaking down and coming apart. One dangerous site of seepage was from the colon—"he was basically pooping into his belly," Jana says. That is deadly.

Now she had to "take out chunks of bowel devitalized from the original surgery." Fixing up the colon took two layers of sutures at each site. Also, the tissue was in such bad shape at this point that Jana couldn't be sure everything she redid would hold. Whatever she accomplished this day might have to be redone later in another surgery.

All that pus was infection that could enter the bloodstream and send Kenzie into septic shock. As we have learned, infection could affect his brain or lungs or heart. Or he could suffer DIC—disseminated intravascular coagulation, in which the clotting system goes haywire, creating clots everywhere.

Jana sliced and stitched for four and a half hours. When it came time to close, she didn't. She tried a method she had never used before—she left part of the abdomen open.

The amount of infection was so vast, only an approach as drastic as a hole left open to the outside could accommodate all that needed to drain out. The half-foot open area did have a "scaffolding" of sutures to ensure that the organs stayed tucked up inside.

After surgery, they wrapped Kenzie's belly in sterile gauze, and injected him with strong antibiotics, pain medications, and lots of fluids. Kenzie was placed on a soft bed in a big run in the ICU.

He made it through the night, but he woke up the next morning suffering. He was weak and in pain. He vomited and wouldn't touch food or water. His heartbeat was irregular. Tucked in the corner run, with IV lines and bandages everywhere, Kenzie did not look like he would survive.

All the while, though, the fluids and meds were working.

Day three was a big one for Kenzie. He stood. He didn't walk; in fact, he wouldn't even take a step. But just getting up was progress. He was in less pain and a lot stronger.

With Kenzie's improvement, a second surgery was scheduled for day four. It was time to "reevaluate the sites." Jana recalls that second operation. "Everything looked great. The tissues were healing. The reattachments were holding. Everything looked pinker and healthier. And there was no smell this time."

Since Kenzie had no interest in eating, Jana inserted a "peg tube" into his stomach so that he could be force-fed directly.

"He needed groceries," Jana says. "These patients really need groceries to make proteins."

This time when surgery was over, they closed Kenzie up completely.

Over the next two days, Kenzie stood, he walked, he even went outside to go to the bathroom. The big black and tan dog who had looked like a dark vision of death was now up and wagging his tail. On the day before Thanksgiving, he got to go home.

It was a great case for Jana. Watching him walk out the doors, she says, "I almost cried."

As it turns out, she didn't miss him for long. Three days later, Kenzie was back in—he had eaten his feeding tube.

Usually, the tube is removed in two weeks, and the site heals on its own. This time Jana decided that if he was healthy enough to have done this, she would leave the tube out.

Months later, Kenzie is perfectly healthy, though Chester said they barely survived the post-operative flatulence. The Gordon setter can walk "three or four miles and is as fit as a fiddle."

"He's a great dog," Jana says. "He's funny and willful, but also incredibly sweet and loving. And the owners' dedication to him and their absolute willingness to see things all the way through is fantastic." That willingness extended to the bill—which turned out to be $6,000.

Now, that's an expensive pair of panty hose.

Treatments for foreign bodies don't always have to be so complicated. Nick Dodman recalls a case from long ago and far away.

He was filling in on weekend duty at a practice in Helensburg, Scotland. The regular vet was "this man called Bob Chesters," Nick says with a smile, "and his wife was called Mrs. Chesters."

Every time Nick started to treat an animal, Mrs. Chesters would pipe up disapprovingly, "That's not the way Bob would do it." Or "Bob always does this," and "Bob says this." Or "Bob wouldn't do that!" "My head was spinning," Nick reports.

On Sunday morning an emergency case came in. The owner said, "The dog's vomiting, vomiting. We think he swallowed a sock."

"So I used his X ray machine, which was out of the Ark," Nick recalls. The beam shone up from under the table, and "I had to lean across, look down through the scope, getting my head irradiated in the process, with some sort of special viewer, like the old protoscopes they used to have in shoe shops where you could look and see your toes wriggling." Nevertheless, he did see the sock and said, "Okay, we have to do surgery."

Mrs. Chesters commented, "Bob wouldn't do surgery."

Nick asked, incredulously, "What would Bob do?"

"Bob would give it apomorphine to make it vomit."

Nick, rolling his eyes, decided to humor good old Mrs. Chesters. "Okay, we'll do what Bob would do," he told her.

Nick administered the apomorphine with a healthy dose of skepticism. "Lo and behold, two minutes later that sock came flying right out, and she looks at me. 'There, that's how Bob would have done it.' "

Nick was astonished. The fusty old practice had taught him something.

A short time later, he was back at a big animal hospital in London. "There was another dog, with a rubber ball in its stomach, and I had an argument with the surgeon. He wanted to operate, and I said, 'Can I try apomorphine?'

"And he said no."

Nick was frustrated. He figured Bob's apomorphine trick would probably work on this case, and he was eager to try it. Then he thought of a medical loophole.

"I said, 'Look, I'm in anesthesia. I am legally allowed to

give whatever anesthetic drugs I want to. I'm going to pre-med with apomorphine.' "

Nick delivered the medicine, and sure enough, the dog threw up. The ball "bounced three times and dropped right into the sink" where Nick was holding the patient.

Now, that's *exactly* the way Bob would have done it.

RESCUE ME

THERE isn't a resident in ICU who hasn't adopted a dog or cat or both. They chose their profession because they love animals, and they are constantly meeting animals who desperately need help. They are suckers for a fuzzy face, a wagging tail, a trauma or disease that will require lots of energy and money (residents don't have much of either to spare, but that doesn't stop them).

Gretchen Schoeffler has two rescued dogs, two rescued cats, and a rescued cockatiel. John MacGregor has made room for three dogs and three cats who needed homes. ICU resident Steve Mensack saved his old lab Topper as well as a cat who was suffering from a fly larva that had burrowed into her head. The parasite species is cuterebra, so he named the now healthy cat "Cutie Reba." He also kept the parasite—in formaldehyde.

Dr. Maureen McMichael is no different. She is constantly amazed by how resilient animals are, particularly her own dog, George.

George, a pit bull mix, was rescued from a dog-fighting ring where he had been used as bait to train more mature combatants. He happened, by luck, to land at the clinic where Maureen was working.

"What they do is take these dogs and string them up on a harness," she says. "Then they let their limbs dangle, and they train the pit bulls to attack their limbs. When they were done with him, they just threw him out of a van."

The animal rescue league found him, and they brought him into the clinic. Vets are accustomed to seeing some brutal sights, but George's wounds stunned them. The poor pup was in shock, too. Bacteria from the bite wounds had invaded his bloodstream, and all his organs were affected.

"When they brought him in, he was in septic shock," Maureen says. "Each leg had about forty-five bite wounds and a lot of pus, really infected. His back right leg was gnawed to the bone—it was just bone hanging." He was in such rough shape any compassionate vet would have to consider putting him to sleep.

"We had him on a table, and we started to have a little conference about him," Maureen remembers. "We decided that even if we could save him physically, which was unlikely, he had no owner, so no one would pay this bill, which would be astronomical. And if we amputated his leg, emotionally he would never be able to recover, and he would never be adopted."

Yet as they were talking, "I turn around and catch his eye, and he wagged his tail. And I thought, 'How can you wag your tail?'"

She smiles at the memory. "To this day, I still don't know how he could have done that. We just joke and say it's because he's so stupid. He has one neuron—a happy neuron—and that's why he's alive today."

They did multiple surgeries on the leg and saved it. What remains most vivid in her mind, though, is the dog's indomitable will. "I certainly wouldn't want to go into a pit bull ring. That would be an awful place, but he is the happiest dog you will ever meet in your entire life."

When Maureen looks back over all the incredible cases she has treated, it is George that affects her the most. "I actually cried for three days at the thought of that happening to an animal. And to know on top of it how very well organized it all was. He had red dye on his neck, and someone told me that they paint them. They do certain dogs Monday, Wednesday, and Friday, and other dogs Tuesday and Thursday, and Saturday, and they have them in cages," she says. "I just couldn't fathom it. I cried for three days—everywhere I went, I would just break down. This is such a sweet, lovely creature who would do nothing but kiss everybody."

Sometimes these animals get saved by residents long after they've been adopted. Dr. Terri O'Toole is renowned for her long-term sleuthing in saving animals, and the case she is best known for is her very own dog, Magic.

Her role, however, was not as primary vet. Many of the doctors in ICU who have their own pets brought to the hospital try not to treat them personally. Their emotions could get in the way of seeing the case clearly. They don't even watch. If another vet is treating their pet, they want that vet to be as relaxed and unencumbered as possible.

Magic, an elderly schnauzer, began to have seizures in the early morning hours while everyone else was sleeping. "I knew what he had the second he started to have seizures," Terri says. "He's a fourteen-year-old dog, and fourteen-year-old dogs with acute-onset seizures typically have brain tumors."

Terri brought Magic in for tests, and the neurologist who examined the dog hoped against hope it wasn't what it appeared to be, for her friend's sake. Terri's guess, though, turned out to be accurate. Rather than being devastated, Terri was philosophical. "I was just hoping that it was a tumor in a place where we could go get it, and it was. I felt pretty good about the whole thing because he's fourteen and if I could have him for another year, I would be happy," she remembers. "But I never anticipated all of the complications."

There would be plenty. In fact, the complications led the veterinary staff down some unorthodox paths, raising dissension about the ethics involved in Magic's care.

Initially, however, there was the straightforward matter of excising the tumor. "The tumor was up in the olfactory lobe," Terri explains, "which is way up front. For dogs it's probably more important than it is for people—the site where you derive your ability to smell."

It was, as far as brain surgery goes, a rather convenient spot. It was, as Terri says, "gettable."

The surgeons at Tufts were not doing much brain surgery and so Terri was sent to a specialist in Portland, Maine. "The surgery went well," she says, "and Magic recovered just fine. He was quite normal."

Five days later, Magic started to stumble and fall, and within hours he wasn't responsive. Terri brought him in, and he had a fever of over 106. A dog's normal temperature range is 100 to 102.5.

"I figured it was infection, because what else could it be?" Terri says. They treated Magic with antibiotics, and sure enough, his fever came down. But the CAT scan of his head showed an anomaly—"he seemed to have something there where there shouldn't have been anything, and it was fluid."

The question was, what was it? The neurologist thought he had an abscess. He called several surgeons, who said that was pretty uncommon, but it does happen. So a second operation was done to remove the abscess.

During his earlier surgery, a medical foam gel had been placed inside the skull to take the place of the tissue that was removed. When the surgeon reopened Magic's skull, he found that the gel had melted into a big mass and there was a lot of fibrous scarring of the tissue in and around it.

He removed that and took a culture sample. It turned out to be a very resistant E coli. He needed an antibiotic that could be injected into the brain. Fortunately, the antibiotic that he had on hand was the one that was needed.

"He did well from that surgery," Terri says, but he seemed strange to her. "His personality was different. The abscess itself was pressing on his frontal lobe, which is where a lot of your personality comes from. And so he now was different—he was goofy."

When Magic came home, Terri says, he started kissing the household cats, which was very uncharacteristic. "He wasn't quite so terrier-like," she says. He had never let her touch his feet before, and now he didn't care.

Within ten days, his behavior changed markedly. "He started to act a little weird, stumbling again, and that progressed over a couple of days." Soon, he was compulsively pacing in circles and wouldn't even look up when his name was called. "That progressed to a pitiful kind of crying," Terri says, "which he had never done before."

Terri looked at her little dog and thought that maybe it was time to end his suffering. He was either in pain or experiencing terrible anxiety. The second surgery did not seem to have alleviated the problem. "To me," Terri explains, "he was showing signs of increased pressure on his brain, and I was going to put him to sleep because I didn't know what was going on."

A CAT scan at Tufts only led to more questions. The ventricles of Magic's brain—the lakes of spinal fluid that bathe the cells of the brain—were enlarged. The ventricles nourish brain cells and take away waste products. Magic's ventricles weren't functioning properly. Oddly, though, instead of being filled with too much fluid, as they would be with hydrocephalus, they were filled with air.

Normally, Terri says, "the brain is constantly making this fluid, and it's constantly draining the fluid out through the spinal cord." The same fluid flows from the brain and down the spinal cord.

With cases of hydrocephalus, in which there is too much fluid in these reservoirs, shunts can be strategically inserted to tap off the excess. But Magic's ventricles were bulging with air, not fluid. It made no sense.

"We didn't know what it was," Terri says. "We didn't know what that disease was. We'd never seen it."

In the meantime, puzzled veterinary neurosurgeons who had been contacted by phone across the country felt the problem was fluid buildup, and they had recommended warm packs on Magic's head to drain fluid through his sinuses. Yet even as Terri followed orders, the amount draining every day was increasing instead of decreasing. Furthermore, it was clear fluid, not full of pus, as a draining infection would be. Nor was Magic getting better. In fact, he was getting worse.

So a Tufts vet phoned her brother-in-law, a neurosurgeon in human medicine at Emory. "Ji Rah's brother-in-law asked us if it was possible that it was cerebral spinal fluid coming from his nose. I said, 'Yeah, it could be, because it's very clear.' And he said, 'This is really bad.' " If brain fluid can leak to the outside, it means that outside elements can get to the brain, which should be sealed off from such exposure. The dog had been sedated, and his head had been propped up. Terri realized that as fluid drained out of his sinuses, air was being pulled up and filling the ventricles.

She likens the dynamic to a medical condition called *pneumothorax.* Often when dogs are hit by a car, the injury allows air to escape the lungs and fill the chest cavity. When the dog tries to breathe in, there is no space for the lungs to expand and the dog's breaths become more and more shallow. "So with Magic they called it a pneumoencephalus rather than hydrocephalus," she says. "His brain was squished because of air."

The brain surgeon at Emory said it was a really bad complication in people, requiring difficult surgery. A catheter would have to be put in to drain fluid out. Culture samples had to be made of everything. One of the layers of the brain had to be closed up. Finally, the defect through the sinus, which the other surgeon had left open, would have to be repaired.

At this news, the surgeon at Tufts said something that many of us have said as a joke: I'm no brain surgeon. He was familiar with the complicated procedure that the medical doctor described, and he was unwilling to take a stab at it. He felt he could only harm the dog.

Calls to veterinary neurologists yielded little. No one was familiar with the problem. Terri reports, "They all kept saying, you need to stop and kill the dog. We don't know what this is."

Weighing in on the other side, meanwhile, was the sister of another vet—John MacGregor. Also a human brain surgeon, she stressed to Terri that this was a medical emergency. Something had to be done quickly.

Terri says she too painted a dire picture: besides all the surgery, the sinuses would need to be packed, and once that happened, the dog would immediately have to go on a ventilator. He'd probably have to stay drugged and on the ventilator for two weeks.

This all added up to putting a very old dog who had already been through two surgeries through a lot more. The neurologist at Tufts listened to all this and told Terri she had better reassess her commitment.

Terri's head was spinning, but while she thought everything through, she made sure Magic was comfortable, giving him ample pain medication.

The next day, she was still in a quandary. John MacGregor's sister was advocating for more surgery, and she said she could easily talk the surgeon through the procedure. But the surgeon wasn't biting. He said no.

Another human surgeon, at the University of Massachusetts Medical Center, was consulted, and he could not believe
that all this strategizing was for a dog. Terri reports that he
said, "You need to reevaluate your ethics." In the end, though,
he agreed to come to Tufts and work with Kim Knowles, another surgeon there.

In turn, Kim voiced her doubts that this was the right thing
to do. Terri recalls, "She says to me, 'You know, this is really
bad. If you want me to put Magic to sleep, I'll put him to
sleep.' "

That made up Terri's mind. Magic was completely doped
up on painkillers, and there were no guarantees that the
surgery would work. Terri thought it was time.

She and Kim walked back to the ICU to end Magic's suffering. But when they got there, an ICU nurse, Kellie Paige,
protested. She had grown very fond of the scrappy little dog,
and she felt he still had a shot.

"So I go to put him to sleep, and Kellie throws herself in
front of the table," Terri remembers. "She's crying, and she
says to Kim Knowles, 'Isn't there something you can do?' And
Kim is saying, 'Don't look at me like that. It's not my fault.' "

In the end, the brain surgeon from the UMass Medical
Center came over to Tufts the next day to do the operation.
He arrived toting a small, wrinkled CVS bag filled with expensive brain surgery equipment. "He brought everything he
would use on a person," Terri says, and he did the surgery he
would have with a human patient. He went in and took cul-
tures—swabbing cells inside the skull to see what kinds of
bacteria, if any, were present. Using a piece of *bovine peri-
cardium*, or heart tissue from a cow, the surgeon closed the
defect that left the brain vulnerable to the outside world. The
skull should be a vault, and now Magic's was again. Also, a
catheter was inserted into the ventricles.

Thankfully, the pressure had already decreased, and the
oversized ventricles had shrunk down toward normal. But it

would take five days for the patch to seal. Magic was kept heavily sedated with his head up.

Nishi managed him through this critical phase. There were plenty of problems to manage. Terri says, "He had a lot of electrolyte abnormalities for a while because of the drugs he was on prior to his surgery." Nishi gave Magic not only simple IV fluids but also a hormone, ADH, or antidiuretic hormone. This was given to him in eye drops that helped his kidneys to concentrate his urine so that he would not dehydrate himself and develop dangerously high sodium levels. After a few days, his kidneys began to concentrate on their own, and he came off the hormone.

Magic is alive today. He is clearly changed, however. His head tilts to one side, and he walks with a strange gait. It's a tippy, unstable kind of prancing movement. He is deaf as well, though that is because of his age, and he watches Terri, who signals him like a flight attendant when she wants him to move in a certain direction.

"His personality is somewhere between the original Magic and the other Magic," Terri reports. "But he's not so goofy. He's not the same dog, but he's pretty good."

Terri says she's learned a lot from the whole ordeal. She has no doubt that trying to take the tumor out in the first place was the right thing to do. But after that, when everything got so complicated?

"Just like so many people with their cats and dogs here, I got sucked into it," she says.

"I was a fool because surgical infection is always a chance. I should have known that that could happen.

"The third complication, the pneumoencephalus, is undocumented in veterinary medicine. So, it's probably a case that needs to get written up, and I think probably we're going to write it up."

She does not think she went too far with Magic. "It was a step-by-step thing, and you had to make decisions. He's going to be fifteen next week. If I have him for a year, this is his normal life span." On the other hand, if she had known initially all that he would go through, she would have declined treatment. "I mean, if that was my choice again, no, I wouldn't. I wouldn't put him through any of it."

Ultimately, Terri feels the experience helps her advise owners as they wrestle with these same situations with their own pets. "They have to make difficult decisions, and it's very subjective because sometimes you do get lucky," she says. "I can easily say to people, 'Believe me, I know what this is all about.' Usually after I tell people a little bit of the abbreviated story, they are feeling so sorry for me, they feel nothing could be that bad."

In our society, we want everything to be perfect. We discard what isn't. Yet Terri can handle the imperfect. At home, she takes care of her two ninety-years-plus, senile aunts.

"Everybody here knows my aunts because I'm always telling funny stories about them. And I noticed that the same doctors who find it difficult to listen to stories about my aunts are the same ones that have a problem with certain animals. And people that have an inability to accept that some people aren't as perfect as other people. Magic is not a hundred percent, but he's good enough. Animals don't have to balance their checkbooks. You don't get disappointed in them if they don't remember their phone numbers. The little things that we find hard to accept in our grandmothers? It's okay in animals."

BAILEY:
THE WONDER DOG

I T was just three days until Christmas, and Kim Deary came home from working at her family's chain of dry-cleaning stores at lunchtime to catch up on wrapping gifts. As she steered her Jeep Cherokee into the driveway, she saw her neighbors' two rottweilers cruising around, but she thought nothing of it. The big dogs were often loose.

Her own dog, Bailey, a beefy but sweet Lab mix, was delighted as always to see her. After their usual greeting, Kim says, she got to work on her holiday chores. Around three she went out to check the mail. With forty acres of woodland around her house and a long driveway, it was a ritual for Bailey to join her and, as she says, "pee on everything on the way." Another part of the ritual is that after the mail pickup, when Kim would reach the front door, Bailey, skittish of the front steps, would scoot around to the sliding glass door at the back of the house and wait for Kim to open it.

This day seemed like all the others. But after retrieving the mail with Bailey, Kim did not find him waiting at his usual spot at the back door. She waited for a second, but still no

Bailey. Almost simultaneously, she heard the screeching of brakes and a horn blowing out front. Heart pounding, she ran to the bay window, scared that Bailey had just been hit by a car. Seeing nothing, she ran outside. That's when she saw, far down the driveway, her dog being dragged away by the rottweilers.

He was howling in terror. Inside the car that had blown the horn was a woman driver who had already dialed 911 on her cell phone to report the incident to the police. At that time of day, school was letting out, and as cars and pedestrians happened by, a crowd formed in an effort to get the rottweilers off Bailey. People threw rocks. They yelled. They blew horns. But nothing would deter these animals from, as Kim says, "ripping at" the terrified and whimpering Bailey. They would stand over their victim, and as soon as Bailey would try to cringe away, they would grab him and start the attack all over again. The violence was, Kim recalls thinking, terrifyingly like that of wildlife in a Serengeti special on the Discovery Channel.

By the time the police arrived, Kim estimates that Bailey's ordeal had already lasted fifteen minutes. Many in the crowd shouted for the officers to shoot the dogs, but that wasn't necessary. For some reason, the dogs simply backed off when the police officers approached.

Because of Bailey's black fur, Kim had not been aware of the extent of the damage. But as Bailey, now free of the rottweilers, ran for home, Kim saw a huge flap of torn skin and muscle on his chest fly open. When she got the terrified dog inside the house, he ran from room to room, splashing blood from gaping wounds that still remained mostly hidden by his fur.

Kim's parents, whom she had contacted during the melee, arrived at her door. With them were two employees from the close-knit staff of the dry-cleaning chain. In two cars, Kim, her husband, her parents, and the two employees careened toward the vet's office. There Bailey would receive some vital care: fluids, which would help replace those he lost through the wounds, and antibiotics, because bite wounds are notoriously "dirty." Finally, he was given pain medication. In the vet's office they could see that all the skin around his neck and shoulders had been ripped open, and his ears remained attached to his head by the tiniest threads of flesh. The doctor's recommendation was to get Bailey to Tufts as soon as possible.

Gretchen still gets teary-eyed when she recalls her first sight of Bailey. "I walked into the ICU, and he was on a gurney, just lying there, and he looked at me and he wagged his tail! That was like, oh, my God, he wagged. And you could see he had all these wounds around his head, but you couldn't see how bad they were because he's a big, hairy fluffy dog."

Gretchen covered all the bases for immediate care and evaluation, "the ABCDs of trauma." The first thing to check is the (a)irway for obstructions. Listening and looking showed Bailey was doing fine on his own. Next is (b)reathing. *Auscultation,* or listening with a stethoscope, proved Bailey was doing fine in this regard, too. (C)irculation is next—a check of the cardiovascular system. Is the heart beating too fast? Does he have a good pulse? Having a look at the color of the gums is a good clue, along with an assessment of mental status. Bailey was a little "tachycardic," meaning his heart rate was a little fast. But Gretchen says that could have been because he "was still a little shocky" or "in a lot of pain." Certainly, he had good reasons for both those possibilities. The normal heart rate for a dog ranges from 60 to 100, depending on size, and in a stressful situation, like a veterinary exam, that can go up to 120 to 140. Finally, (d)iagnosis and drugs: determine his injuries and plan a course of action.

She took a blood sample when she placed an intravenous catheter to see if he'd had significant blood loss. Next, Bailey was given fluids, as at the vet's. "We usually give them fluids, knowing he's lost a lot of body fluids, and is also suffering from shock. Animals in shock have low blood pressure and usually need volume. And we start antibiotics for the open wounds—you start those IVs. Then you get the wounds cleaned once he's stable."

The night of the attack, Kim and her anxious entourage spent from six to nine o'clock alternately in the waiting room or in examining rooms talking with the staff. Gretchen laid out how grave the situation was and how costly the care could be. To Kim, there was no question, no hesitation. Everything must be done to save Bailey.

The family was sent home, and Gretchen got to work. Fortunately, it was a relatively slow night in the emergency room, and she was free to spend a good deal of time with Bailey undistracted while another resident, Alison Gaynor, held down the fort. All in all, Gretchen would work more than six hours fighting to save Bailey's life. She knew full well that even if she could lead Bailey safely through this dangerous short-term period, he would still be vulnerable to deadly infections over several weeks of recovery.

With trauma, such as the animal bite wounds Bailey suffered, vets identify three danger zones in the time line of trauma and recovery. In the book *Veterinary Emergency Medicine Secrets*, edited by Wayne Wingfield, they are listed as: (1) within minutes of the trauma; (2) the first three to four hours, in which "prompt, aggressive treatment can make a difference in survival"; and (3) after three to five days, when great attention must still be paid to recovery, and during which hidden injuries may reveal themselves.

With a fourth-year veterinary student to help out, Bailey was anesthetized. "We started shaving," Gretchen says, raising her eyebrows at the memory. "We shaved and cleaned for two to two and a half hours. We used clippers and tweezers to pick hair out of the wounds. And then we trimmed away devitalized tissue or dead tissue.

"He was a bit of a jigsaw puzzle. It was difficult to figure out how best to put things back together. It took a long time.

"One ear was ripped in half; half the pinna [the flap itself] was gone. So I just trimmed away the cartilage because it was sticking out. But the skin won't grow back over that, so I trimmed it and then sutured the skin to itself.

"On the other side, the ear was actually pulled off his head. So you couldn't see where it belonged. You could see the cartilage was torn, you just couldn't see where it went. So I just tacked it to the top of his head to try to approximate about where it would go." Gretchen shakes her head, amused by her plastic surgery skills. "When the swelling went down, I realized it was a little higher than on the other side. Ari kept telling me it would give Bailey character, and that he wouldn't mind."

The task was backbreaking. "We worked on that dog from nine-thirty till three in the morning. A long time. A lot of surgery."

In Bailey's file, early that morning after all the surgery, Gretchen wrote, "Bailey is very lucky to be alive. Certainly not out of the woods yet." Up above, the stark terminology of the medical file sums up his condition on arrival—"massive, severe wounds."

After surgery, she had started him on hetastarch, a special fluid that can help maintain adequate fluid volume within the blood vessels. It also helps maintain blood pressure and decrease fluid leaking from the blood vessels. Gretchen explains, "We knew he had lost a lot of the protein, and was going to have a lot of exudation [oozing fluids], almost like a burn patient would. Ari took over his primary care the next day and realized he was going to be sicker than I had originally thought, probably, and expanded the antibiotic coverage, afraid that he was going to become septic."

Bailey might not have made it. The severity of his wounds, the amount of punishment his system had taken, the chance for infection, all stood against him. When such a large body surface area has been wounded and exposed to so much contamination, an army of white blood cells comes to the area to clean things up. Those white blood cells release what are called inflammatory mediators or chemicals. That recuperative effort can have bad effects, called the systemic inflammatory response syndrome, or SIRS.

In human or animal hospitals, it's all too easy to lose a patient this way, even with the most sophisticated equipment. The most highly skilled staff can only stand by watching helplessly. "There isn't a whole lot we can do," Gretchen says, "except keep them on high rates of fluids to keep things flushed out, to keep things excreted. You try to reduce the amount of bacterial toxins produced by reducing the bacterial level with antibiotics.

"And then you just wait and hope. You hope that the body's self-defense mechanisms can take care of it but not overdo it."

The next day, Bailey lay in a morphine haze in his cage. Gretchen warned Kim that the next time she saw her dog, he would look very different. "Both ears were nearly ripped off," she wrote in her report. "We did what we could to save them."

From the shoulders up to his eyebrows, he was shaved bare, and the swelling gave this lab mix the profile of a sharpei—drooping eyes, pendulous jowls and neck. Stitches crisscrossed his shaved skin. Yellow rubber drains protruded everywhere, like fingers protruding from his flesh.

He was patched up for now, but Gretchen knew that down the road, as his skin scarred up and pulled, he would probably need more surgery. Most of all, he looked excruciatingly sore and terribly, terribly ill.

He wore a fentanyl patch on his inner thigh, which continuously delivers a pain medication through the skin. Fluids and antibiotics were continuously pumped into his beaten body. The urine collecting in a bag from his catheter was a sickly brown.

Ari sized up his new patient in the record. "Condition given as critical, but potential for a good quality of life if above complications can be managed or avoided."

The "above complications" were various forms of infection and their own complications. Bailey's blood glucose was dropping, which meant he might be developing an overwhelming bacterial infection, or sepsis. It could also indicate *leukopenia*, or low white count, also seen in sepsis.

Ari's counterattack included antibiotics and fluids; a dextrose drip to keep Bailey's glucose level normal; coag profile, which checks the coagulation system (as sepsis develops, this usually becomes abnormal and patients may require medical therapy such as plasma transfusions); and increased monitoring. Bailey needed to be watched carefully.

Bailey's system was overloaded with bacteria. He had severe cellulitis, which is purulent material in the tissues; loss of blood proteins (in sepsis, blood vessels leak protein, so the protein level in the blood goes down); hypoglycemia, since low blood glucose goes hand in hand with sepsis; and a decreased white-blood cell count. Consumption of platelets and clotting factors was detected as well.

Early in the evening, Bailey was able to stand for the first time, but he looked weak and in a great deal of pain. He did not take a single step before lying back down. Food and water did not interest him.

Although Bailey was now officially a case for Ari Jutkowitz, Gretchen stopped by to see him that December 24. "Oh, Bailey," she said, "what a rotten Christmas." He looked like he needed a miracle. Bailey could hardly lift his swollen head, and he seemed to be in pain even when he blinked his sad brown eyes at Gretchen.

For Ari, this would be a case that tugged at him emotionally from the start. Ari says his favorite cases are those with a medical puzzle to figure out, a dog who may be flat out, but will still wag his tail, and owners who are willing to work hard with you. Bailey had it all.

"He was a great case for all those reasons. He's a great dog. And he was a dog who would have died," Ari says. "We didn't know for days if he was going to make it. We were watching and not knowing, but wishing."

"Circumstances made it easy for me to fall for Bailey," Ari says. First of all, residents sometimes have days off right in the middle of a case. But in Bailey's case, Ari says, "I was on for nine days in a row. So I had him from start to finish."

That afternoon Ari took Bailey to "dirty surgery," or the non-sterile surgical area, and cleaned out all the wounds—on his face, neck, chest, and legs—with warm water. He flushed extensively with sterile saline solution, plus a diluted wash of betadine. With care, he spread Vaseline around the bases of the drains protruding from his head and neck.

Ari gave the patient plenty of fluids, colloids, dextrose drips, antibiotics, and a double dose of pain medication—both morphine and fentanyl. He was also given Heparin to prevent further clotting problems.

When Kim visited Bailey on Christmas Eve, it was hard for her to see her dog with his wounds so exposed. Ari talked with her about the extent of Bailey's problems and the worsening of the local infection and cellulitis. Kim was just grateful that Bailey was alive this Christmas Eve, and she knew he was getting great care. She left the hospital hoping her boy would be fine.

Bailey was a little "brighter," seeming to notice what was going on around him more. His temperature was climbing—102.2—but was still within normal range. His respiratory rate was higher than normal.

In his notes that night, Ari wrote of his concerns. He saw infection brewing, and even though the blood tests weren't bad, he felt they would be shortly. "Grave concerns about sepsis, SIRS, DIC, but these have not manifested yet on blood work."

On Christmas Day, Kim came to visit in the afternoon. Blue-eyed, with auburn hair, she was a glamorous Santa Claus, bringing chocolates, cookies, cupcakes, and a red and white Christmas bread for the staff and dog and cat treats for all the patients in the ICU. Smiling and effervescent, Kim couldn't stop saying how happy and grateful she was that Bailey was still alive.

He did look better. His face was still very swollen, but it was coming down. His heart sounded okay—no murmur. But his lungs sounded a bit harsh. It was hard to see Bailey in this condition, and Kim was teary as she left.

Once she was gone, Ari kneeled down in front of Bailey's open cage to clean him up a bit. He gave the dog a quick shot of morphine to keep him comfortable during his bath.

Ari used sterile gauze soaked in Chlorhexidine disinfectant to gently clean the many wounds. The resident looked concerned at a black patch of skin on Bailey's head and said, "He may lose that." It's necrosing, or dying, tissue—skin that didn't get the circulation back. While Ari lightly scrubbed the swollen and oozing skin, Bailey looked skyward with a mournful expression.

After the procedure was over, Bailey lay in his cage. His head was upright but kept sagging down, and his heavy eyelids just wouldn't remain open. The poor dog struggled to stay alert as the morphine pulled him into slumber.

The day after Christmas, when Kim visited again, Ari had a gift for her—Bailey seemed better. Though he vomited a bit after feeding at six a.m., he has been doing fine. At ten a.m., he walked outside to go to the bathroom, and his urine was a healthy clear yellow. Once back inside, Ari placed soothing hot packs on Bailey's swollen face and cleaned the wounds with Betadine.

Despite being zonked on painkillers, despite the pain and swelling, Bailey went out several times during the day. His heart seemed pretty good and his lungs sounded a little better than the day before.

Ari allowed himself a little optimism in his notes. "Overall looks great—consider reducing fluids, spreading out pain meds." Best of all, he mulled over this thought: "Possibly move to wards tomorrow." A graduation to the wards would mean that Bailey was well enough not to need constant monitoring any longer.

More problems were to follow.

The next day he developed a "gallop rhythm"—his heart was beating too fast. The sepsis, or bacteria invasion, had affected his heart. It was probably *endocarditis*, a bacterial infection of the heart valves.

"He had gotten septic," Ari explains. "When that happens, it affected the way his heart was working so his heart wasn't pumping appropriately. So his heart wasn't able to handle all the fluids he was getting."

Despite the problem, Bailey seemed more comfortable and his appetite was coming back. At ten that night, Ari cleaned Bailey's face and debrided, or removed, dead tissue. Hot packs were again applied to his swollen face. Ari also removed a few of the crusty drains. Some areas were healing nicely while other patches of tissue were darkening up and dying. Ari thought some of the stitched-up areas would have to be reopened and "explored."

They used echocardiography "to see exactly what the heart was doing. [It seemed to be] a problem of volume and decreased contractility of the heart and not a bacterial problem so we cut back on the fluids."

The amount of Hetastarch and other fluids was reduced, and they hoped that Bailey would drink enough water on his own.

By December 28, Bailey's swelling came way down. It was

the first time Ari felt confident that his patient would make it. His face, though still bare of any fur, now looked like a Labrador's. Still, little worrisome patches of skin kept turning up black—it looked as though another surgery was inevitable. Bailey was still droopy from all the pain meds. "He's pretty well gorked," Gretchen says.

On December 29, Bailey was allowed to drink water, but his food was removed so that his stomach would be empty for surgery. The reduction of fluids seemed to have resolved the problem of Bailey's gallop rhythm. His swelling was greatly reduced and the dog looked like a Labrador retriever again. He was healing, and Ari continued to keep the wounds clean and to debride all the dead skin to help the process.

By December 30, Bailey was ready for a second surgery. He went outside early in the morning to go to the bathroom, and his walk, Ari says, was almost "sprightly." His heart was getting better and better, and his pulse was strong. There was some pus oozing from a drain near his left ear, and there was one stubborn patch of dead tissue on his right cheek. But he was stable, and this second surgery was an important step in his recovery.

While under anesthesia, dead tissue was aggressively removed from around his wounds, and new, clean drains replaced the old ones. He came through surgery fine, and that meant he would be able to go home the next day.

At five-thirty in the afternoon on New Year's Eve, Kim Deary arrives at the hospital with good cheer. She gets to take Bailey home today. Always stylish on her visits, Kim is wearing a buttery soft gray leather jacket and toting a lipstick red patent leather bag. Generous as usual, she is carrying two big shopping bags with gifts for everyone.

It is a special day, and Ari has even come in on his day off for it.

There's chocolate for the staff. But Gretchen and Ari receive even more. For Gretchen, Bailey's newly anointed fairy godmother, there is pixie dust and a little fairy statuette. For Ari, there is a cardboard top hat for New Year's and a little black stuffed puppy with a red chenille scarf that looks just like Bailey. "Except the stuffed dog's ears haven't been stitched on crooked," Gretchen notes. She promises Ari she can "fix" his new toy.

Kim's visit has made everyone happy, especially Bailey. When he is led into the examining room where Kim is waiting, he breaks out in a smile for the first time in the hospital.

Ari goes over Bailey's condition and what Kim will need to do at home.

"We cultured Bailey's wounds in surgery," Ari tells her, "and they're growing some bugs [bacteria]. Which we expected. Some bacteria will probably be resistant to the antibiotics, but we'll have the culture back shortly."

Ari explains that the wounds need to stay as clean as possible, and that hot compresses applied to Bailey's face with a kitchen towel three times a day will help the healing process by easing drainage.

"Everywhere where there's puffiness and wounds," he instructs, "you should loosen the debris, and get it to drain out."

Ari explains to Kim that Bailey is still very uncomfortable. The tender-hearted resident tells her, "Be patient with him. He may or may not let you do everything you need to do. He does sometimes sort of snap at us a little when we touch his drains."

Bailey will need to continue taking antibiotics at home, and he should have his activities restricted, only going out for short walks to go to the bathroom. Ari cautions Kim to call if Bailey becomes lethargic, or vomits, or if he refuses to eat.

Bailey will need to come back in if his incisions become red or inflamed. Because of infection and the severity of the wounds, some incisions could possibly open.

Kim looks at Bailey. "Will you give me kisses? Want to go for a ride?" At the magic word "ride," Bailey tilts his head and paws her hand.

Just then Gretchen pokes her head in the room and tells Kim, "He really is a special dog." Then she turns to Bailey. "I'm going to miss you. Now, stay out of trouble."

Ari tells Kim that Bailey should come back in two weeks to get stitches out, and Ari will evaluate then whether Bailey will need further surgery. As the scar tissue heals, it shrinks, and there is a chance Bailey's eye will get tugged in the process.

Kim looks at her beloved dog, whose head is stitched like a baseball, and says, "My boyfriend's back."

Bailey paces to the door. He knows its time to go home.

Ari hands Kim her home instructions typed up. At the bottom, he has written of Bailey, "He has been a wonderful boy, and all of us here will miss seeing him around."

Once more Kim looks at Ari and says, "I just can't thank you enough."

Ari turns red and looks at Bailey. "All right, Bailey, you can go home."

As Kim walks Bailey to the front door, heads pop out of examining rooms and from around every corner. Everyone shouts, "Bye, Bailey!" as they see him heading home.

Ari follows them to the waiting room and stands, teary-eyed, as Bailey and Kim disappear out the front door. Ari says of his career, "I don't have any big plans. I'd love to discover something that changes medicine. But, really, it's the individual cases I'll look back on. If for one dog, I made some owner happy, then I'm happy."

Clearly, he's already met that goal today.

Ari's last glimpse is of Bailey's black tail wagging along as he trots next to his owner. Of that moment, Ari will say later, "When Bailey finally left the hospital, well, it was the best feeling I can remember."

LESSONS OF THE ICU

T'S easy to imagine what a gift it is to owners like Kim Deary to have a beloved pet returned home from the brink of death. But what the animals give back to the ICU doctors is something much harder to define. The veterinarians say that the value of their work can't even be put into words. Yet they know they have been forever changed by these experiences.

Ari feels he has been transformed. He says that growing up, he was extremely competitive scholastically. He even skipped a year of high school because he was "so goal-oriented." "I always wanted to be the best at the hardest thing," he says.

But somehow what seemed a basic component of his character has shifted. After just a few years as a veterinarian, he reports, "I get gentler and sadder the older I get and the longer I'm here. And I don't know if that's animals teaching me or me realizing there are things I can change and things I can't." His goals now include things that cannot be easily measured.

He isn't alone. "I think I would like to be able to say at the end of my career that I haven't forgotten to give love to the animals and to the people," Dr. Maureen McMichael says. The sentiment is echoed by Lisa Powell. "I hope I can say that I helped a lot of animals not only live but also die with dignity, and that I helped the owners."

The animals seem to teach simple lessons about life.

"I think animals bear hardship and disease and pain with more dignity than maybe people do," Dr. John Berg says. "It may be that they don't understand it as much—we don't know to what degree animals feel pain as compared to humans, that's impossible to know—but they seem to be better patients and they tend to bounce back from surgery incredibly fast." That zest for life is a joy for a doctor to witness, and John wonders if physicians would be happier if their patients "had the personality makeup that our patients do."

For many, the task of caring for these innocent creatures can be somewhat of a sacred duty. A mission of healing. "I do feel entrusted with their care," Dr. Nishi Dhupa says. And what she has received in return is truly immeasurable.

It would be impossible to calculate how much the animals have taught her, but Nishi says it is immense. "Animals continue to surprise me with their patience, their level of tolerance, and their strength," Nishi says, "but most of all, with their ability to *forgive.*"